# BEYOND CHARITY

# BEYOND CHARITY

## THE CALL TO CHRISTIAN COMMUNITY DEVELOPMENT

## John M. Perkins

**Baker Books**

A Division of Baker Book House Co.
Grand Rapids, Michigan 49516

Published by Baker Books
a division of Baker Book House Company
P.O. Box 6287, Grand Rapids, Michigan 49516-6287

Printed in the United States of America

Unless otherwise noted, all Scripture references are taken from the HOLY BIBLE, NEW INTERNATIONAL VERSION®. NIV®. Copyright © 1973, 1978, 1984 by International Bible Society. Used by permission of Zondervan Publishing House. All rights reserved.

Scripture references designated NASB are from the New American Standard Bible, © the Lockman Foundation 1960, 1962, 1963, 1968, 1971, 1972, 1973, 1975, 1977.

Scripture references designated KJV are from the King James Version of the Bible.

**Library of Congress Cataloging-in-Publication Data**

Perkins, John M., 1930–
    Beyond charity : the call to Christian community development / John Perkins
    p.   cm.
    ISBN 0-8010-7122-4
    1. Church work with the poor—United States. 2. Community development—United States—Religious aspects—Christianity.
I. Title
BV639'. P6P44'  1993
253', 09173' 2—dc20                                                    93–18862

# CONTENTS

# ACKNOWLEDGMENTS

This book is affectionately dedicated to those who have helped me over the years:

The poor and common people in Mendenhall, Mississippi, from whom I learned so much.

The wonderful friends in Jackson, Mississippi who helped to shape the visions.

The many friends in Pasadena, California who supported me morally, spiritually, and in many other ways to help my life become more stable, including the Board of Directors of the John M. Perkins Foundation: Howard Ahmanson, William Grieg, Roland Hinz, Jeff Cotter, Addie James, David Evans, Bud Ipema, Michael Mata, Pearl Morris, Norm Nason, Derek Perkins, Naima Quarles, Roy Rogers, Harold Spees, Gary Vander Ark, Alfred Whittaker, and Daniel Woodard.

The Board of Directors for the Harambee Christian Family Center: Stan Lazarian, Jerry Bacon, Clifford Briggs, Carlos Caldwell, George Comfort, Richard Culpepper, Dorothy Ertel, Betty Jo Ford, Maxine Gebbie, Joel Heger, Addie James, Eva Meyers, Dinah Roberts, Linda Schultheis, and Claretta Smith.

Wayne Gordon and the Christian Community Development Association have enriched my life.

Dennis and Margaret Howard for their kindness.

I now want to acknowledge those who labored with me throughout this project. Without them this book would not have been possible: Patricia Warren, Rodolpho Carrasco, and Catherine Hirshfeld.

I do not want to forget my son Spencer and his wife, Nancy, and Chris Rice for their tireless editing of the manuscript.

To my wife, Vera Mae, mother of our eight children, who has been by my side from the very beginning.

# INTRODUCTION

For a brief moment in May 1992, many Americans following the shocking events unfolding in inner-city Los Angeles may have felt that the American dream was on the verge of becoming an American nightmare.

Adding to the fear of Americans was the cry from many other inner cities that their communities were only one incident away from a similar outburst. L.A. was an urgent wake-up call for all of us—a warning that if not heeded will cost us much more than the welfare programs of which we have already grown weary. Behind the South Central L.A. eruption, and beneath the surface of urban America, is a long, downward spiral that cries out for a response from Christians.

The civil rights movement was a mostly peaceful protest within the bounds of the Constitution. By contrast, the 1960s riots were a glimpse of what this country had to look forward to if the civil rights movement produced no change. Many historians believe the fear of this anger finally forced the government to act.

As a result, laws were passed to eliminate segregation; jobs and training programs came into being; and numerous government programs were set up to deal with the poverty that was the legacy of racism. During the 1960s those of us who were upwardly mobile benefited greatly. We were able to obtain education and skills, which afforded many of us good jobs for the first time.

Ironically, however, eliminating these injustices helped to create the situation we have in the inner cities today. As a result of the Fair Housing Act of 1968, many upwardly mobile blacks began seizing this new opportunity to move up and out of the inner city. Armed with new jobs that moved us into the middle class, we left the community behind, buying homes outside the neighborhood and returning to the area only to administer programs for the people still living there. This made it difficult for those who had moved out to identify with the pain of the urban poor. Their jobs depended on the poor, making them "poverty brokers" of sorts.

One of the casualties of this exodus was black-owned businesses. Many children of small-business owners, after they were educated and employed, moved out of the neighborhood. Consequently, parents had no one to whom they could pass on the family business. When they got older, they began to sell these businesses to new immigrants who saw the opportunity to make a livelihood by supplying goods and services to the black community.

This out-of-the-ghetto migration by black leadership—pastors, businessmen, teachers, and professionals—left the uneducated poor behind. The moral and spiritual restraint provided by the leadership of the middle class was no longer present.

Well-intended welfare laws also backfired. Americans have always assumed that strong families are the basis of society, but we have not as a nation developed a family policy. Before welfare, it took a two-parent family to survive. Now the single mother with children, helped by programs like Aid to Families with Dependent Children (AFDC), anchored the new economy of the inner city. Despite good intentions, AFDC has helped to forestall and break up more black families than anything since slavery's auction blocks sold husbands, wives, and children in different directions. Sadly enough, it also provides much of the revenue for the inner-city drug trade.

In the 1970s, 50 percent of inner-city black children were born out of wedlock. (Today it is more than 60 percent.) With no male discipline, too many children were left to roam the neighborhoods and make their own lives. Gangs became a substitute for the family unit. Schools could no longer handle these children and began to neutralize their presence by putting them in slow-learning classes. With little expected of them, 11- and 12-year-olds began dropping out of school.

The erosion of moral and spiritual values, which plagued every level of our society, had an especially devastating effect on our cities. Our government leaders' interpretation of the separation of church and state, especially as it related to the schools, opened the doors for an amoral society.

The downward spiral continued with the introduction of crack cocaine into the equation. Gangs began to take over the drug business, and frustrated single mothers, supported by welfare or earning money from prostitution, became the number one customers. This meant going to jail and, even worse, neglect of children. In an ironic way, drugs kept a lid on the anger and frustration of our urban poor. Had it not been for the introduction of the drug trade into our cities, I'm convinced that this explosion would have happened much earlier.

One more element contributed to the plight of the urban poor. And this element—materialism—escapes all the analysis I've read of the urban situation. Throughout this country, you are what you own or, in the case of the poor, what you rent to own. The ills of our society at large are all magnified in the poor community, including materialism. Television is the means by which this disease gets transmitted. Even the poorest of the poor have access to a TV, and they watch more TV than anyone. They are constantly bombarded with all the "stuff" that characters and advertisers say living the American dream should include. Therefore, over the past thirty years, it has become much more frustrating to be poor in America.

Today's black urban youth are like explosive powder kegs: without the disciplines of strong families or community, constantly told by society that materialism makes life worthwhile, perceiving middle-class Americans as having everything they can't have, seeing police as just another gang out to get them. And all this anger is given definition by the latest urban preacher, the rap artist. All that is needed is one racial incident to set them off.

In confronting these conditions, it is much easier to build a new prison or enact a new welfare law or give someone a handout than it is to develop the person. So far, we have settled for the impersonal and the bureaucratic. But, as we are seeing now, in the long run these Band-Aids will be much more expensive than we ever imagined.

I believe there has never been any serious thought given to a comprehensive community-development plan that enables the people to own their neighborhood. The economic development that flows from ownership would reward individual initiative, causing people to look inward instead of to institutions "out there" to solve the problem. Instead, the only hope is moving up and out.

   The desperate conditions that face urban America call for a revolution in our attempts at a solution. Over the course of my thirty-
five years of living and working among the poor, I have come to
believe that these desperate problems cannot be solved without strong
commitment and risky actions on the part of ordinary Christians with
heroic faith who believe, as the little shepherd boy David did, that
our God is greater than any Goliath that dares to mock his name.

   God has always depended on his people to step onto the battle-
field, to assume responsibility, to take the lead, and to make his love
visible to an unbelieving, mocking world. Indeed, I would have to
deny God's work in my very own life to say there are no solutions to
this great challenge of the poor that faces America today.

   I was born into the grinding poverty of the Mississippi of the
1930s. Over my years of struggling with racism and poverty, and
then over three decades of trying to live out what I have come to call
Christian community development, it is God's movement in my own
life that inspires me to face with hope the crisis of America's poor.

   My struggle began one Sunday morning in 1957 at a little Holiness Mission in Pasadena, California, when I discovered that God
loved me. I had grown up in Mississippi without a mother or a father.
I grew up without the certainty of love. That morning all the long-
ing of my heart came together when I heard that God loved me, that
God had sent his Son into the world to die for my sake. That morning, the best that I knew how, in the midst of all my feelings of inferiority, in spite of the fact that I was a third-grade dropout, at the age
of twenty-seven I reached out to God. It seemed that this was the
morning that I had been born for. I felt what I had missed all of my
life: I was loved by a holy God. I felt great joy mixed with sadness
and guilt. I could not stop weeping, for I was overwhelmed by my
foolishness and sinfulness. I saw that my sin was like spitting in the
face of this God who loved me even now in spite of my sin. I felt that
I had been rejecting him for twenty-seven years. And yet I was over-
joyed at the experience of God's love for me. The experience of this
joy has stayed with me ever since.

   Over the last thirty-five years, the struggle has been to reconcile
what happened to me there, the experience of God's love, with living in the world. The struggle has been to show to my neighbor the
reconciling love I found at conversion, when out in the world I

found bigotry and hatred—even from Christians—because I was black. At every key point, at every critical moment, I have been surrounded by Christians who loved me so that I felt that reconciling love. And at those crucial moments, many of those people who have loved me have been white. Because of their love for me, I learned that without our hands, without our feet, God has no way to touch the world of need.

This has been true from the beginning of my pilgrimage. Mrs. Willie Price, a friend of my wife who was a youth Bible teacher, told me about a Tuesday night Bible study. The first time I went, I looked around me and saw that everyone there was white except me. I had never, ever, seen white folks and black folks together in church in Mississippi, so I was afraid I might get turned away; but my desire to know the Bible was too strong for me to leave.

I went to the back of the room and listened to the Bible lesson from there. By the end of the lesson, I knew I wanted to keep coming to this class. I knew I wanted to learn what this teacher had to teach me, but I was afraid that I would not be wanted, because I was black. I waited until most of the other men had left, and then I went up to the teacher. I reached out to shake his hand, but he didn't shake my hand—he put his arm around my shoulder. I felt the reconciling love of God. I felt that he wanted me there.

This teacher, whose name was Wayne Leitch, took me under his wing and began to disciple me. He taught me how to study and love the Word of God. He taught me ways to study so that I could understand the Bible; and he believed that I could understand; he believed in me. He gave me a hope that I had never had in my life and told me that someday I would be speaking to thousands of people. I was a stumbling young man, full of fear, but somehow, deep down inside, and without telling anyone else, I embraced the hope that someday I would be able to share the precious Word that this former Child Evangelism leader established in me.

Then there was the Christian Businessmen's Committee, where men like John McGill also nurtured and discipled me. At that time I was the only black attending, yet I felt accepted and loved within this Christian community in a way I had never felt before. I had experienced racism and bigotry as a boy. I had watched as whites murdered my own brother. I had watched all types of brutalization back in Mississippi, but here was a group of white Christians encouraging me in my newfound faith. I can remember Dave Peacock who loved me so dearly, Ed Anthony, and others who were very conservative Christians, but who put their arms around me and loved me. And I loved them back.

When God called me back to Mississippi, these men were my first supporters. They would come to visit me from time to time while I was there, and they got their congregations involved with the work I was doing in Mississippi.

In 1960, Mendenhall, Mississippi, was a poor rural area growing poorer as local sharecroppers were losing their jobs to advances in farming technology. The racism that was a part of Southern culture meant that dwindling employment opportunities hurt blacks most. Many left Mendenhall, vowing never to return. Those who remained saw their children leave, looking for better lives elsewhere.

God opened a marvelous opportunity for Vera Mae and me to go into the public schools and share the gospel with 15,000 children every month. At the same time, the civil rights struggle was beginning, and Vera Mae and I and our neighbors were involved. There were young men who brought teams of young folks to help us, like John MacArthur Jr.; they became involved in the struggle, too. In fact, John was with me in Mississippi in 1968 when Martin Luther King Jr. was killed. I witnessed how his life was challenged as he understood racism and bigotry anew, as it was inflicted on him, a former Bob Jones University student. And through all this I, too, was struggling with the reality of knowing God's reconciling love while in the middle of all this hate.

Somehow in the midst of all the racial chaos the Mendenhall Ministries began. John MacArthur Jr., along with Dave Nichols, the registrar of Los Angeles Baptist College (now Master's College), helped me get young people, like Dolphus Weary and his future wife, Rosie Camper; Artis Fletcher and his future wife, Carolyn Albritten; and my own kids, in Christian colleges. We started a day-care center, youth program, church, adult education program, thrift store, and health center. Then, after twelve years, those young people, armed with college and seminary degrees, began to return to their community to work and to live. Their love for God had given them a burden to return and heal Mendenhall, rather than run and escape. The ministries we developed had formed an economic base and provided opportunities for employment.

As indigenous leadership began to develop in Mendenhall, a group of us moved to Jackson in 1972 to start another ministry there—my family, a white family (H. and Terry Spees), and Herbert Jones, one of the young men who had been converted in Mendenhall. We began to put into practice what we had learned in the previous twelve years, living out the reconciling love of God in another community. And God blessed us.

As we settled into Jackson, a series of articles about me appeared in national magazines like *Time, Jet,* and *Sojourners.* I guess my reputation preceded me into the city, because in Jackson, for the first time, we met local whites who were willing to join with us and provide resources to us—people like Victor Smith, Stuart Irby, Cobby Ware, Paul Fowler, Phil Estes, Sam Patterson, and others. So with national and local support, a ministry began to develop in Jackson, called Voice of Calvary Ministries. Housing, health care, thrift stores, investment corporations, and leadership development outreaches began to develop soon after. A church—Voice of Calvary Fellowship—was planted and became the heart of our life, working hand-in-hand with our community development ministries.

I began speaking throughout the United States. Voice of Calvary Ministries emerged as a leader in Christian community development—a model of blacks and whites living, working, and worshiping together.

As we began to share this vision around the nation, other ministries began to sprout up. A young white Moody Bible Institute graduate named Glen Kehrein relocated into the Austin neighborhood of Chicago and started Circle Urban Ministries. He was eventually joined by a black pastor, Raleigh Washington. Wayne Gordon, a young white Wheaton College graduate, moved into Lawndale, one of Chicago's more severe ghettos, and started teaching public school. From that a ministry developed, Lawndale Community Church, which provides all types of services from a church base. More than thirty youngsters from Lawndale Community Church have graduated from college, many returning to their community to head up ministries there.

Bob Lupton, a young Youth for Christ worker, went to Atlanta and began to see and understand what was happening to the young black boys there. He became burdened and came and spent time with us in Mississippi. I remember him saying, in the midst of tears, "We have got to do more than just share the gospel with them [the youth in the urban areas]; we have to do something about the quality of life these young people are living." Out of that burden has come Family Consultation Services (FCS) Urban Ministries in Atlanta, which is pioneering in housing and the "reneighboring" of the deteriorating Summerhill community, future site of the 1996 Olympics.

Kathy Dudley, a young white woman mentored by Dolphus Weary, moved into the deteriorating West Dallas community and began working with the children there. Her ministry, Voice of Hope, is truly about bringing hope to the hopeless.

In 1982 I moved to Pasadena, California, planning to retire and spend my time writing and speaking. However, God called, and Vera Mae and I, with my son Derek, started the Harambee Christian Family Center amidst Northwest Pasadena's difficult conditions of crime, drugs, and family breakdown.

We also watched other ministries continue to emerge from all around the United States, like the Jesus People in Chicago, Neighborhood Ministries in Denver, the Church of the Messiah in Detroit (led by Ron Spann), and Emerald City Outreach Ministries in Seattle. I saw all of these young men and women trying to live out the reconciling love of God, responding to the love they had felt from God in their own lives just as I had responded to his love in mine.

All of us began to meet together and talk about starting an association of ministries. Voice of Calvary's Lem Tucker, the Mid-America Leadership Foundation's Bud Ipema, businessman Malcolm Street, I, and others took leadership with this idea. So many of my dear friends came alongside at this time: Howard Ahmanson, Roland Hinz, Norm Nason, Steve and Stan Lazarian, Bill Grieg, Herbert West, Bill Hoehn, Gary Vander Ark, Chuck Colson and Prison Fellowship, James Dobson and Focus on the Family, Ted Engstrom and World Vision, the Pew Memorial Trust, the Stewardship Foundation, and many others. All of these people and organizations helped and supported us.

And so in 1989 the Christian Community Development Association (CCDA) was born. Through CCDA, committed people of God working in the trenches among America's poor began to discover that they were not alone. Our individual stories of God's faithfulness began to be woven into a rich, broad movement of God's Spirit, bringing hope and love to broken people and their communities. The ministries and churches and families of CCDA are showing that it is possible for the church to live out the love of God in the world; that black and white, Jew and Gentile can be reconciled; and that we can make a difference, that we can rescue the ghettos of this nation.

Finally, in 1991 God laid another burden on my heart. I was heartbroken by the negative way we as blacks are portrayed in the media, especially at how even our own portray our young blacks as overly sexual, violent, and criminal in films such as *Jungle Fever* and *Boyz N the 'Hood*. It disturbed me that there was no Christian voice in the media directed at the problems in the inner city, that called African Americans to high moral standards, that went beyond blame to responsibility, that talked not just about victimization but about hope and progress and taking advantage of the opportunities that we have today that did not exist thirty years ago, that did not focus solely on the divisions between races but encouraged reconciliation.

Out of that burden, *Urban Family* magazine was born: a credible, quality, national Christian magazine devoted to building up urban families. Once again, God prepared the way for action through a friend, Roland Hinz, who offered his expertise and support. As the Black Muslims go to the street corners with their *Final Call* and the Jehovah's Witnesses move door to door with their *Watchtower*, now Christians, too, have a powerful printed voice that offers a message of life-changing hope to urban families, creatively pointing them to Jesus Christ.

From one humble Mendenhall storefront to a national magazine, and from one family's tiny vision in rural Mississippi to the hundreds of committed families and ministries that make up CCDA—as I look back on this history of God's faithfulness I am full of hope. But it is crucial that the source of that hope be named, for only hope that is sure can give the long-term vision and endurance needed to tackle the problems of urban America.

It has been said over and over again that the government has tried to solve the problems of the inner city and has failed. Yes, the government has failed when it comes to the poor. Our nation's cities are in a crisis. But in every crisis there is opportunity. I believe that this crisis is an opportunity for us, the church, to step forward and lead the way in restoring the inner city by bringing the physical presence of God into the city. I believe that the church has the opportunity to pioneer and model a way of life whereby our nation itself can experience a new birth. One of the reasons that I love this country is because of its commitment to freedom. That freedom gives us, the church—the people of God—the opportunity to demonstrate to the rest of the world a more excellent way.

To offer hope to the desperation of urban America that we saw reflected in the flames and looting of Los Angeles in 1992, the church must be at its best. I submit to you that the time is absolutely right. It is time for the church, yes, the whole church, to take a whole gospel on a whole mission to the whole world. It is time for us to exhibit by our very lives that we believe in the oneness of the Body of Christ. It is time for us to prove that the purpose of the gospel is to reconcile alienated people to God and to each other, across racial, cultural, social, and economic barriers. It is time for the reconciling love of God that has touched each individual heart to spill over into love for our neighbor.

This book, then, is an invitation for you to join us in this struggle—to join with the other members of our association, to join with the urban people of God, to make Christ's Body both visible and credible. It is an invitation for you to help us lead the way in bringing hope to the broken communities of our nation. By doing this, by going beyond charity to reconciliation and development, we can become a lamp hanging on a post, which gives light to a dark world.

# PART ONE

# OUR VISION

# 1

## BEYOND CHARITY

We live in a critical hour in which the "least among us" (Luke 9:48) are growing at a frightening rate. We can no longer see pain and suffering as something that takes place "over there" in Third World settings. We now hear the cries of our own people, especially those in our urban centers. The urgency that I feel is the force that lies behind this book.

Of course, poverty is not limited to our urban areas, but this new breed of poverty—a poverty compounded by dependency and hopelessness—has nearly everyone scratching their heads and pretending not to notice. Growing up in the sharecropping system and living among the poor now has caused me to experience and internalize the physical and emotional hardships that accompany this relatively new breed of urban poverty. I have also seen others who have come to help internalize our suffering, making our struggle their own. While those relocating to the streets of the inner city have not been overcome by the physical and emotional hardships that the urban poor face daily, they have been so captured, spiritually, by our struggle that they are unable to walk away freely.

Indeed, Jesus was foretold as the one who would choose to identify with our suffering, bringing laughter where there is despair, light where there is only darkness, joy where there is only grief. He, himself, was a man, "despised and rejected by men, a man of sorrows, and familiar with suffering" (Isa. 53:3). My hope is that we will con-

21

tinue to look to Jesus and his example to provide us with ways to bring healing to the crushed spirit.

## The Current Climate of Need

In this country, the current climate of need that leads to this hope-lessness is visited disproportionately on African Americans. Three centuries of exploitation, dehumanizing laws, and now dependency and the absence of moral leadership have produced a situation that only the presence of God can overcome. I'm sure, by now, you have heard all the statistics:

- Infants born to black teenage girls have a 50 percent higher mortality rate than those of the general population
- 50 percent of black teens are unemployed (triple the rate of whites)
- 25 percent of black men aged 20 through 64 are unemployed
- One-third of blacks live below the poverty line
- 25 percent of black males aged 16 through 30 are in our prison system
- 64 percent of the prison population is black (and yet blacks account for only 12 percent of the general population)
- 600,000 blacks are in prisons, as opposed to 400,000 in colleges
- Two-thirds of black children are born to unwed mothers
- 2.6 million of our 4.6 million black families are headed by single women
- Homicide is the leading cause of death for black males aged 15 through 44
- Homicide is the second cause of death for all black males under 70

I have not written this book to condemn the history of exploitation that so effectively harmed millions of God's children. Others have spoken more clearly and forcefully than I ever could. Rather, I have written for *Christians*, liberal or conservative, Democrat or Republican who, by their lives, are attempting to illustrate a Christ-like tenderness for those with a crushed spirit. This book is a call to all Christians to make their lives more meaningful and living demonstrations of the gospel of Christ.

If we are to link hands and work together and concentrate on the real needs of the urban poor, then it would be helpful if we understood some obstacles that prevent us from getting at real solutions.

## The Obstacles to Solutions

### *A Charity Mentality*

America's best intentions, most sincere thoughts, noblest efforts—all of these are useless to the urban poor if they do not connect with our personally defined, deepest felt needs. In fact, acts of charity can be dangerous because givers can feel good about actions that actually accomplish very little, or even create dependency. The result is that their sense of satisfaction takes away any motivation to seek more creative long-range development strategies. Overcoming an attitude of charity is a difficult task because it requires givers to demand more of themselves than good will.

In the days immediately following the L.A. riots, we witnessed an unprecedented outpouring of Christian charity. Thousands of pounds of food and clothing were given by people whose hearts hurt for those who had to suffer due to the events of May 1992.

Christian charity should never be discouraged, and there will always be a place for acts of sharing and kindness, but charity is only a beginning point, not the final strategy or solution. South Central L.A. certainly needed food and clothing, but much more important for the people there is a long-term commitment to development.

Many times we give because we don't know what else to do. We see the suffering and we have to do something, but we should always be sure to keep the focus of our giving on the ones who need the help. Sometimes our giving is motivated by guilt. When this is the case, we are giving for selfish reasons—to make ourselves feel okay. This can be very dangerous for the poor. Today, many poor people will check your motives by asking you to explain why you are doing what you are doing. If they feel they are being used to ease your own pain, their distrust will deepen.

As Christians, we need to rethink the way we do charity. If the past thirty years have taught us anything about the poverty mentality it is that undisciplined giving can be just as destructive as the poverty it was meant to alleviate.

## Racial Polarization

A second obstacle to real solutions for our new breed of urban poverty is that race has divided us so efficiently into separate churches, neighborhoods, relationships, and agendas, that there is hardly the opportunity for the whole church to attack the problem of urban poverty. It is sad that more than twenty years after the civil rights movement, we still have to talk about racism.

David Claerbaut, a white sociologist, maintains that "while whites cringe at notions of black power, they have casually accepted white power as a way of American life."[1] We prefer holding to this reality to the possibility of adjusting the system in ways that would lead to a setback in status.

It is unfortunate that race still plays a powerful role in the out-workings of our Christianity. Few of us have escaped the destructive legacy of racism in this country. It has had a lasting effect on all of us. As Christians, looking through the eyes of Christ at the problems facing our inner cities, the skin color of the poor should be irrelevant. But this is not the case. It is sad but true that many white Christians look at inner cities, see black or brown, and label the problem as "not my fault" and "not my responsibility."

Blacks make up 64 percent of our total prison population, although we are only 12 percent of the national population. White America can look at a statistic like this and draw two possible conclusions: Either blacks are somehow innately inferior to everyone else, or there is something innately wrong with our society. Somehow whites (sometimes even white Christians) are too often able to read the statistics and conclude that their racism is justified after all: "Just look at the evidence!" But can you imagine Jesus having this thought? There is absolutely no justifiable grounds for accepting one race as superior to another. The conscience of the Christian church should be pricked after reading such deplorable statistics, leading us to take action to correct the inequities.

Because race has been such a major player in our history, any attempts to solve the problems of our cities will mean, first, acknowledging the race problem instead of denying that it is a factor and, second, planning our strategies to anticipate the wild card of race. Otherwise race will continue to be an obstacle with enough emotional power to divide and conquer.

## A Victim Mentality and Self-Doubt

Another obstacle that stands in the way of black development is what author Shelby Steele calls our own "self-doubt." His brave book, *The Content of Our Character*, has drawn much fire from the political left. I believe his thesis needs a fair hearing; Steele does not underestimate the profound damage that historical white racism brought to us. He is, however, concerned with the present, and it is his view that our consciousness of being victimized as a group has prevailed over our determination to progress as individuals. Centuries of abuse have left us with a deflated sense of self. Rather than aspiring to the challenges that integration has offered us, we forego these opportunities for advancement and instead complain about our status as victims of race, fearing that we might fail to achieve in the new arena of opportunity.

Says Steele, "I think they [African Americans] *choose* to believe in their inferiority, not to fulfill society's prophecy about them, but for the comforts and rationalizations their racial 'inferiority' affords them."[2] It is unpopular, says Steele, for blacks to let go of the "victim of white racism" label. The *group*-consciousness they have achieved as blacks demands it. Whites do not think of themselves primarily in terms of a racial group-consciousness, so they are free to pursue individual advancement.

These tough words for blacks suggest that we have accepted the image of an innocent victim of racism and the only way out is entitlement at the white's expense. As long as we cling to a "victims" label, it will be difficult for us to assume individual responsibility and to advance. "Whites must guarantee a free and fair society," says Steele. "But we blacks must be responsible for actualizing our own lives."[3]

The only way through this self-imposed paralysis is to confront the doubts and take on the risks of achieving. The stakes are high, because when a white person fails, it is an individual event. When a black person fails, it serves to reinforce the historical message to him or her and to white onlookers that, indeed, the African-American race is inferior.

It is true that we have inherited the option to accept government charity simply because of our race. Consequently, the notion of black-as-victim is nurtured and the idea that society "owes" certain hand-outs and hand-ups persists. Regardless of what position you take, be it right or left, we as individuals and as a race will not be successful in giving the leadership that is necessary to establish a social, economic, and religious base for our people unless we are willing to swallow doubt, take the risk, and move forward.

### Government Programs

Although bashing our nation's welfare system has become a popular political pastime, we need to take a good hard look at the results of the government's war on poverty. Conservatives contend that this overgrown bureaucracy was the attempt of liberal whites to alleviate their guilt for years of oppression. Whether this be true or false is of very little consequence to the poor. The question that we should all be asking ourselves is, "Have these welfare programs substantially improved the lot of the urban poor?"

The most expensive, and probably the most destructive program, was the Aid to Families with Dependent Children (AFDC). This program assumed that there was no family in place, and so failed to include the basic elements that would affirm and rebuild the family. It attempted to stabilize the mother without the father in the home. It did not allow the extended family to become part of the support system. There was no incentive for enterprising individuals to remove themselves from that system. Therefore, the system perpetuated itself.

In many cases even today this "aid" has become something like a birthright, sort of a "rite of passage" for young girls—an inheritance to be claimed when you come of age. Settling for this so-called benefit has allowed single-parent families to become the norm in poor communities instead of the exception. Eventually young males growing up without the positive discipline of a father become angry and violent because of the humiliation of "living off their mothers."

In my neighborhood, the first day of each month when the women receive their government checks is sarcastically referred to by some young men as "Mother's Day." Even in this tension-relieving humor you can feel the sting of anger and humiliation. This shame and humiliation cause these young boys to grow up to physically, financially, and emotionally exploit women who to them are just like their mothers.

My son Derek teaches a Bible study each Wednesday at 4:00 P.M. in one of the apartment complexes in Northwest Pasadena. I am continually amazed at how a hush comes over the room, and how all the kids are attentive, when he, a black male, is conducting the class. One afternoon he was unable to go, so my wife went to teach in his place. I went along with her and sat in the back of the class as she told a wonderful Bible story. There were twenty children present, fourteen girls and six boys. The girls listened attentively, but at least five of the boys did not hear anything that my wife was saying. Their emotions, limited attention span, preoccupation with hitting each other, wiggling, and so forth, caused them to not only ignore what was being said, but to disrupt the entire class.

This class illustrated to me the rebellion of those young black boys against female authority and domination, and many people around the country are beginning to see the same pattern. More than eight out of every ten kids we work with come from broken families, the majority headed by females. We have prisons, parole offices, and morgues full of young black men who have become violent and exploitative because of this cycle. The mothers then are left in the communities alone with the children and, to compound a bad situation, usually live in congested government-sponsored housing. The destruction of the family is inescapable.

Since I live in an urban area, I know only too well how a program that should be a safety net is actually discouraging initiative, rewarding dependency, and reinforcing racism for both blacks and whites. Charitable motives or not, the present welfare system as it exists is not good enough. We need a system that reflects the excellence of a nation that can engineer sophisticated space programs, water-delivery systems, transportation wonders, computer technology, and smart bombs. To insist that we hold on to the welfare approach because it came from a charitable heart is to insist that the charitable feelings of the giver are more important than the real needs of the poor.

## Overcoming the Obstacles through the Church

I believe there is only one group of people in society who can overcome these obstacles. God's people have solutions that are qualitatively different from any other approach to the poor. The best that God's people have to offer is relationships with the poor that reflect the kind of careful, quality attention we have in our own families. This is the high quality of relationships offered by a people seeking to "love their neighbor as they love themselves."

Giving is a dangerous business because, as Robert Lupton puts it, "*Receiving* is a humbling matter. It implies neediness. It categorizes one as being worse off than the giver."[4] Therefore, we must be careful how we give. Giving should affirm and not dehumanize. We give because God gave to us. We should be humbled by our opportunities to give. A gift is something that you value yourself, something that you would want to receive yourself.

This concept of giving is one of the greatest challenges facing the church in the days ahead. The church's efforts in Christian community development must go beyond charity. They must go further than acts of kindness. Somehow we have to disconnect what and how we give from our need to feel good about ourselves. The plight of the urban poor is a problem that belongs to all, and the church's witness and credibility are inextricably tied to this plight.

The partnership that has developed between us at the Harambee Center and the people at the Santa Ynez Valley Presbyterian Church[5] is an excellent example of how churches can support urban ministries. Jeff Cotter, the former pastor of that church, felt a burden to get involved with our ministry at Harambee. He initially approached Jim Elam, the missions chairman, and as a result of their interaction, Jeff, Jim, Jeff Bridgemen (the new senior pastor), Dean Broyles (the youth pastor), and others from the church came to Pasadena and spent the day interacting with me and the Harambee staff. This wonderful group of people listened as we discussed with them our most deeply felt needs and how they could assist us. Out of that has evolved a healthy relationship with that whole church.

Their financial support to us is generous, yet they are involved in many other ways. As we purchase houses to expand our base in Northwest Pasadena, they are there to assist. Our young people go camping together in the mountains and visit each others' homes. This type of commitment goes beyond just giving money and visiting the ministry site once a year. Despite being located in a secluded valley near California's central coast, this church is taking concrete steps beyond their comfort zone to real relationships that uphold us in the work of developing indigenous leaders in Northwest Pasadena.

Such is the call of this book. We in the church cannot separate our Christianity from the hopelessness of the urban poor. If so, then something about the gospel has failed us. Indeed, when our Christian faith is confronted with the reality of the urban poor, we are challenged by significant questions that go to the very heart of the gospel: What should Christian community look like in an hour such as this? What should the body of believers look like? What are the marks of an authentic church in an hour such as this, of a church responding to the poor? Finally, in writing this book, I am moved to ask, in the words of Francis Schaeffer, "How then should Christians live?" In the following pages, I hope to raise our expectations of each other, encourage us to persist in our most noble calling, and point to new directions that indeed can make a concrete difference in urban America.

# 2

# FROM QUICK FIXES TO FELT NEEDS

Fresh out of a prestigious university, Eddie was a highly motivated young man who thought he had a solution to the problems in
the urban community. Eddie made many contributions to my own
life while he worked with me. However, Eddie thought the urban
community's problems could be "fixed" in one or two years. When
he realized that his solution could not "fix" the problems, he moved
on to a successful career with a large New York advertising firm.
There, ironically, he used his skill as an advertiser along with what
he learned about the poor during his time in the urban community
to further exploit the poor. As we blacks consume more alcohol,
more tobacco, more television, and more movies than other Americans (many of these consumables corrupt the morals and the health
of our people), Eddie is right alongside us, exploiting "the market"
for cold profit, contributing to the problem he once tried to solve.

## The Quick-Fix Illusion

Eddie is an example of those who try to take the quick-fix approach
to the plight of America's poor, which is not a problem to be solved
quickly and painlessly. It takes time to develop and grow what our
urban communities need most: indigenous leaders. Quick-fix solutions cannot truly develop people.

The quick-fix mentality sets up a "we-them" dynamic: "We do-
gooders have the solution for these poor people." This attitude

assumes that somehow those who do not live in the urban community already know what urban people need. But it is only when we really come shoulder to shoulder with the people at a specific spot in urban America that we can begin to discern ways that the gospel will become meaningful in that context. With the transformation of "you, them, and theirs" to "we, us, and ours," we will understand most clearly the real problems facing the poor; then we may begin to look for real solutions.

The quick-fix mentality also allows urban activists to think they can fix people. Bob Lupton, head of FCS Urban Ministries in Atlanta, says:

> I'm beginning to see that fixing people is a dangerous business. Fixing assumes that I know what the final form should be, as if I were a spiritual orthodontist who knew just what wires need tightening to produce the perfect smile. When I presume to fix someone, I shape that person with my values, doctrine, hygiene, parenting, vocabulary, housekeeping, nutrition and a whole host of things. Fixing is license to fashion after my image one who may be uniquely created to flower in quite a different form. It is a dangerous business because it may block or skew the growth of another. And it may unwittingly intrude on the work that God reserves for himself alone. [1]

It is clear in Scripture that God works constantly to transform people who then reflect the fruit of the Spirit. People go wrong when they assume that they know what needs fixing. Some things, like child neglect and abuse, dropping out of school, and the breakdown of the family, obviously need fixing. But if you don't live in the urban community and allow it to become a part of you, you might see what needs fixing but you won't understand the reasons these problems have developed. This lack of understanding will make your approach irrelevant.

Sometimes people from the suburbs come to my neighborhood, take a look at the trash on the street and sidewalks, and say, "What this place needs is a cleanup campaign." So they go around the neighborhood trying to get people to join a cleanup campaign. Then, when no one joins in it with them, they say, "The problem here is that no one cares about keeping the neighborhood clean."

Sure the neighborhood needs cleaning up. But this need is only a symptom of much deeper needs that, left unaddressed, will return the neighborhood to its former state a few days after the cleanup campaign is over. When people have no hope for their community's betterment, or even their personal betterment, it is manifested in many ways. Because there is no vision of ever owning the businesses on their streets or the houses they live in, they see no point in going to school or working, so days are filled with shooting dice on the sidewalk. "When there is no vision," says the Bible, "the people are unrestrained" (Prov. 29:18 NASB). The subtle temptation to address the surface needs is quite understandable. The neighborhood can be successfully cleaned up in a weekend, but tackling the problem of how to instill pride in a community and how to have ownership of it takes a long-term commitment.

Finally, the quick-fix mentality causes the activist to hurriedly focus on what is obviously wrong and consequently miss seeing all that is good and wonderful in the urban community. Drugs, unemployment, crime, and children without fathers will and should capture our attention. But, because time is limited, the quick-fix activist will not see the joy, the laughter, the love of children, the storytelling, the natural beauty, and untapped potential of the children. The tremendous spiritual resources and the resilience of old saints who have discovered how to live the hope of Christ in crushing circumstances will be missed. Being able to see and experience these qualities will inspire and encourage the hearts and souls of those of us who are working to build God's kingdom among the urban poor.

When Vera Mae and I first moved back to Mississippi, we had to do whatever we could to make ends meet during that first year of ministry. I began working, picking cotton to feed my family. The people gave us sweet potatoes, corn, peas, buttermilk, eggs, and milk. When I was locked in jail, those same people came and put up their property to get me out. When the law enforcement and Klan types tried to drive me out of town, these people came and guarded my house at night. A significant bond of trust develops when a leader is dependent on the people, and the people see themselves as part of that person's survival.

Instead of coming with a quick-fix solution, more suburban people of all races need to hear and answer the call of God to put themselves in direct, personal relationship to the urban community in order to discover the felt needs of the people. The most effective way to do this is by living among the very people that we have been called to serve. By discovering people's felt needs for ourselves and making their needs our own, we can begin to help bring about real, lasting change in our urban communities.

The great question in indigenous leadership development is, "How do we affirm the dignity of people, motivate them, and help them take responsibility for their own lives?" By beginning with people's felt needs we establish a relationship and a trust, which then enables us to move on to deeper issues of development. This idea of beginning with people's felt needs is summed up in what I call the felt-need concept.

## Jesus Talks with a Samaritan Woman

Jesus' encounter with the Samaritan woman at the well (John 4) shows us a pathway to a deeper relationship with the poor.

For a Jew, the Samaritans were the outcasts, the throw-aways of society much like the ghetto dwellers of today. When Jews went up to Galilee from Jerusalem, instead of taking the more direct route that led through Samaria, they would take the long way around. But Jesus chose to go directly into Samaria. Going to the tough places usually requires an intentional decision. The challenge is for us to ask God, "Is there a Samaria that you are calling me to go into?"

When Jesus meets the Samaritan woman at the well, he knows her immediate (felt) need is for water from the well, and he does not ignore this need in order to meet her deeper need for eternal life. His first words to her were not, "You are a sinner; you need to accept me into your life; God loves you and has a wonderful plan for your life"; or, "If you have enough faith you can drink all the water you want."

Instead, Jesus says to her, "Give me a drink of water." He did not start by saying, "I can help you." He wanted her to know that she could help him. The Jews despised and separated themselves from the Samaritans, so by talking to her and asking her for help—demonstrating she had something of value that she could share with him—Jesus affirmed her dignity and broke down the wall of distrust.

There is a great barrier of distrust between the rich and poor today, which can be overcome only by affirming the dignity of people and loving them around their needs. During more than thirty-five years of ministry, we have discovered that one of the needs we can love people around is their children. As we love their children, the parents begin to respect us and to look to our spiritual motives.

Now this Samaritan woman, who understood the historical relationship between Jew and Samaritan, needed to understand Jesus' motives. Motives are very important to the people who are being helped. What drives us to go out of our way and show compassion for someone in need? The poor are experts at sniffing out guilt and exploiting it. She asks, "How is it that you, being a Jew, ask drink of me who am a woman of Samaria, for the Jews have no dealings with the Samaritans." She raises the race issue, and believe me, if she had smelled guilt motivating Jesus, she would have exploited it. But because Jesus has won her trust by going out on a limb and talking to her and affirming her, he can cut through the old racial garbage. He says, "If you knew the gift of God and who it is that asks you for a drink, you would have asked him and he would have given you living water."

When she hears "living water" she right away says, "Sir, you have nothing to draw with and the well is deep. Where can you get this living water?" Jesus has identified her felt need, and now he will show her that she has a deeper need. He will not say to her, "You are a sinner" but rather will love her into discovering her need herself.

Jesus replies, "Everyone who drinks this water will be thirsty again, but whoever drinks the water I give him will never thirst. Indeed, the water I give him will become in him a spring of water welling up to eternal life." She responds, "Sir, give me this water so that I won't get thirsty and have to keep coming here to draw water." Once Jesus had affirmed her around her felt need, he was then in a position to show her her deeper spiritual need. Because Jesus had won her trust and she now believed that he loved and cared for her, they could get down to the heart of the matter. It is at this point that Jesus says, "Go, call your husband." When she answers that she has no husband, and Jesus acknowledges that she has had five and is now living with a man who is not her husband, he takes her to a deeper level of understanding, leading her to say, "I know that Messiah is coming."

Answers Jesus: "I who speak to you am he." The woman returned to her city and brought many people back with her to meet Jesus; many of the Samaritans believed in him.

Jesus goes directly to the people and loves and affirms them. Because they trust him, many come to believe in him. Jesus' method of ministering to people around their needs offers us a powerful example. Jesus met the Samaritan woman around her deepest felt need (having her dignity affirmed), loved her around that need (by starting an unheard-of dialogue), made her need his very own (asking for a drink), then shared with her the "wonderful plan" by helping her discover for herself her deeper need.

## Ministering Effectively

There is an old Chinese poem that illustrates the felt-need concept very clearly:

> Go to the people
> Live among them
> Learn from them
> Love them
> Start with what you know
> Build on what they have:
> But of the best leaders
> When their task is done
> The people will remark
> "We have done it ourselves."

Felt needs are different from person to person and place to place, and in order to do ministry effectively you will need to discover and identify these needs. Over the years we have found, however, that there are three inherited needs that are universal. The extent to which a person has these needs met is the extent to which that person develops, grows, and secures a sense of dignity.

The first need is *the need to belong*. We all have a need to belong to someone and to something. In the poorer areas of our nation, families are often torn apart, love is scarce, and people live with a sense of hopelessness and with a bitterness toward life. They want to belong, but feel like the world all around them, on the streets and in the home, is a hostile place. This need to belong is at the heart of the urban gang problem.

In my community in Northwest Pasadena, 84 percent of the children live without a father at home; one year only three of seventy children enrolled in our after-school tutoring program at the Harambee Center went home to a father and a mother. The family is so fragile in my community that one of our main goals at Harambee Center is to try to become a second family to these children, which puts us into direct competition with the drug dealers and the gangs.

The second need is *the need to be significant and important*—to be somebody. As we develop indigenous leaders we do it in a way that affirms the dignity of a person. We try to motivate people to take responsibility for their own lives. It is the opposite of the welfare mentality, which cripples people and makes them dependent on others. It is amazing how these children, who hear and experience so much negative reinforcement, thrive when they begin to believe that they are special.

The third need is *the need for a reasonable amount of security*. Many of our cities, like Northwest Pasadena, are not secure places to live. Shortly after returning from duty in the Persian Gulf, a young soldier was killed by a stray bullet from a drive-by shooting in Los Angeles. Our cities are in terrible shape when a soldier is safer on the front lines of a war than he is in his own home. If our Christian community development is to be successful then a major focus of our work must be to make our families feel secure in their own neighborhoods. One of the most gratifying things for me is to see the children, who used to live in terror, begin to play in the streets again.

To meet these needs, we practice "the three Rs of community development." These principles, described in detail in my book *With Justice for All*, are at the heart of our strategy for living Christian community development.

The first "R" is *relocation*—moving into a needy community so that its needs become our own needs. For some of us, relocation means "going back," as it did for Dolphus Weary, who grew up in the poverty of Mendenhall, got a taste of success outside, but responded to God's call to return to his hometown with his skills and leadership and give his life to the people there. For others, relocation means moving from the outside in, to uplift the people who live there.

The second "R" is *reconciliation.* The love and forgiveness of the gospel reconcile us to God and to each other across all racial, cultural, social, and economic barriers.

The third "R" is *redistribution.* Christ calls us to share with those in need. This means redistribution of more than our goods; it means a sharing of our skills, technology, and educational resources in a way that empowers people to break out of the cycle of poverty.

## The Example of Wayne Gordon

Living out the felt-need concept is just the reverse of the quick-fix mentality. Wayne Gordon's life is an outstanding example.

Wayne grew up in a part of Iowa where there were hardly any blacks. He went to Wheaton College and ended up exploring Chicago during and after his schooling. He did an internship one summer in the city and felt the hurt of the inner city. Upon graduating he felt called of God to come into the city and be a teacher, as he was trained to be, in an all-black school in the ghetto.

Wayne did not just get a job teaching at the school. He actually moved into the city, near the school where he taught. He became the school's wrestling coach and began to share his faith and to interact with the young people. From that he started a Bible class. But he did not stop with evangelism. He put some gym equipment into a little storefront and began to run a gym.

Out of that little storefront he helped develop Lawndale Community Church, which is today at the cutting edge of Christian community development ministry. Their health center, with a staff of fourteen doctors, a dentist, and an eye doctor, sees about 24,000 patients a year. They are developing affordable housing to help increase the number of individual homeowners in the community. They also operate a clothing outlet and a gymnasium. Lawndale is doing more today in terms of indigenous leadership development than any ministry I know about in America. Recently they established a scholarship program, guaranteeing college scholarships to thirty-five young people who discipline themselves and complete Lawndale's development program.

Today, Wayne (or "Coach" as he is called by the young people) has been joined in ministry by a black brother, Carey Casey, who is the shepherding pastor at Lawndale Church. Besides being the church's outreach pastor, in 1989 Wayne was elected president of the Christian Community Development Association. Wayne has been able to accomplish all that he has because he was committed over the long term. He has won the trust of the people. He knew that Lawndale's problems would not be fixed by quick solutions but that solutions had to be worked out over a period of time.

A little while after moving into Lawndale, Wayne met Anne (who had just graduated from Taylor University) and married her; she joined him in the community. The very night that they moved into their apartment, they returned from a party to discover that their house had been burglarized. That was seventeen years ago. If Wayne had entered Lawndale with a quick-fix mentality he probably would have left soon after this burglary. But he didn't leave. Although he has had twelve more burglaries since that time, and expects that there will probably be more, he has no intention of leaving.

The stories I could tell about people like Wayne would fill another book. Wayne and Anne Gordon are great examples of the kind of people our urban communities need. Despite their white skin, they are sensitive to the felt needs of their community because they have made that community their own. Now when there is a drug house that is threatening the kids of the community, it threatens their own kids too. When the neighborhood suffers from a lack of quality health care, it is a problem for Wayne and Anne too. They have earned the trust and respect of their neighbors because they are committed for the long term. When asked why, Wayne replies, "I'm just trying to love my neighbor as I love myself."

# 3

# THE MARKS OF AN AUTHENTIC CHURCH

One of my favorite places to be on Sunday morning is at Rock of Our Salvation Evangelical Free Church in the inner city of Chicago. I love the inspirational music of their choir, white and black rocking side by side to the sweet chords of black gospel music, lifting their voices in praise to their common God. I love to look around the gym where they worship, picturing the scene during the rest of the week when the room is filled with young men from the community playing basketball. I love to listen to the prayers—from affluent white college students seeking God's help in their studies to the struggling mother on welfare asking the Lord to help her find a job, from the black middle-class family seeking the strength to be a light to the drug dealers on their street to the young teenager crying out for guidance to reach his peers in gangs for Christ.

The reason I love Rock Church is because in the midst of these unlikely partners in worship, the true mission of the church is being fleshed out. You see, the church is the Body of Christ. It is to literally be the replacement of Jesus in a given community, doing what he would do, going where he would go, teaching what he would teach. The church's call is to be the one place in the world where Jews, Gentiles, and all other races are reconciled into one body. Local congregations should reflect local ethnic diversity; our churches ought to show that the followers of one God live together as one people in fellowship with that one God.

## A Divided Church

As I look at the universal church today, I see it being divided broadly along three different theological ideals, which have produced three different forms of the church.

Thanks to the zeal of European missionaries and to the historical, political, and intellectual power of Europe, European theology is the most dominant theology in the world today. But the legacy of that theology is bittersweet. While many of these missionaries were courageous, faithful pioneers who brought the message of the gospel to foreign territory at great personal sacrifice, often their theology and their actions separated love for God from love for neighbor. The result was that their theology accommodated the subjugation of nonwhite peoples through colonization, slavery, Manifest Destiny, and other forms of domination, rather than repudiating it as unbiblical. Many European thinkers today continue to do theology within that framework, making it difficult for them to see, understand, or speak out against oppression.

European theology was a theology of liberation for Europeans. In fact, it motivated many Europeans to come to this country. America was to be the place where European Christians could be liberated from the oppressive European governments that suppressed their religious expression and conscience. In America, they could serve God as they pleased.

But the liberation Europeans took for granted for themselves was not extended to the native Americans who were already here and whose land was taken by force, nor was it extended to Africans, who were brought here by force to work the land. In spite of that, we Africans took on our oppressor's religion. Upon close examination, our black forefathers found that a proper reading and living of "the Book" did indeed mean liberation for everyone, including them. Because the European theology would not accommodate our liberation, we created our own form of the gospel. We cried out in the words of the old spiritual, "Go down Moses, way down in Egypt land, tell ole Pharaoh to let my people go." This is the origin of black theology, born in rebellion against European theology.

Like all theologies should be, it is a theology of liberation from oppression. But liberation to what? Back to Africa? To integration?

Black theology has never adequately answered this question. There has always been the question of what liberation should look like. It is the same question that must be answered by the black Christian leaders of South Africa in response to the reality of a post-apartheid South Africa. For black people, the gospel became a gospel of protest. Black theology is an expression of and response to white oppression.

Finally, there is Latin American theology. As Latin American Christian leaders living among the poor looked at their world, they saw oppression in the form of colonization through military governments and dictators who dominated the countries' resources and sold their countries' natural wealth to the industrialized countries for their own individual profit. Control was maintained through military power sanctioned by the benefiting industrialized countries. Latin American Christians who loved the poor began to see the gospel, not communism or capitalism, as the best way to liberate people from oppression. Thus, the birth of liberation theology. While restoring a sense of God's love for the poor and desire to see them liberated from economic and physical oppression, liberation theology has often stopped short of a strong message of spiritual liberation.

## The Need for a New Theology

Today the church is divided among these three theologies: European theology, black theology, and liberation theology. The problems in today's church reflect this division along theological lines. The white suburban church in America today has largely failed to answer the call of God for justice for the poor and oppressed. Orlando Costas, Latin American missiologist, comments on a visit to an Asian slum: "How is it that the ruling elite can be satisfied with the dehumanization that occurs in these slums? How have religious communities in general and Christians in particular allowed themselves to become so dehumanized that they can go to sleep peacefully despite the millions around them who live and suffer in the shantytowns of the world?"[1]

Not only is the slum dehumanizing to the people who dwell there, but our failure to respond to the slum is an indictment on the church. As Christians, our love for a just God should cause us to act when we see the crushed spirit of the slum dweller. "How can Christians be content with a church in which the very heart of the Christian faith and calling is ignored?" asks Costas.

I have known many Christians who left the suburban, middle-class congregations they grew up in to serve the urban poor. Unfortunately, many of these urban workers live out their faith among the urban poor *in spite of* their home congregations. Because of their relocation to these places of pain, they have suffered criticism for being irresponsible ("Your parents spent $80,000 to send you to college for *this?*") and even rebellious ("Have you become one of those radical social gospel types?"). Usually these workers are led to the urban poor by a desire to answer what they see as the true calling and mission of the church. But many end up living out their Christian faith unsupported by the very congregations that ought to be nurturing and sustaining them.

Black congregations today are failing just as much as white congregations to address the alarming problems of the inner city: the growing hateful and materialistic mentality; the violence committed by our young people who kill each other for a pair of sneakers; the continual filling of our children's veins with drugs. Yet while we talk a lot about the problems—we protest them loudly—we still seem to expect someone else to do the solving.

As blacks, sometimes we are very slow to speak out against our own people for fear of alienation from them. As Richelieu Richardson observes, "It seems we now will accept anything, be it good or destructive, as long as it doesn't come from a white hand. Shoot me—Dope me—Oppress me, My Brother! Blackness is the mitigating factor. . . . In an Atlanta housing project, several black young men are led to a playground and murdered, execution-style, by rival drug gangs. No marches, no riots, no nothing! These types of incidents are commonplace—ask any cop who patrols the inner city."[2]

We blacks have been fighting for justice so long that what has been done to us versus what we've done to ourselves gets blurred. As a black man who has worked for years to make life better for my people, I'm convinced it's time for a revolution in our thinking. Today, I believe the time has come for us to refocus our energies on things we can change for ourselves.

We might not be able to change the hearts of racists, but we can refuse to let their attitudes affect our behavior. We can't force people of another race to give us jobs, but we can as a people determine to control our own economic future. We can't change our painful history of oppression, but we can decide that we'll not submit to the shackles of our past.

Yes, there are still barriers that need to come down and attitudes that need to change. But we have won enough opportunity to begin shaping the future for our children and our community. We must take leadership and make it our responsibility to reach out and bring the healing power of God to the inner city. We must reach out to the needy because some of the neediest people in America are our own people.

Both white and black congregations have been slow to address the problems of our urban poor. For the most part we have ignored this call from our cities. What, then, should be the call upon the church? What should the church be doing? What alternative are we providing to the three theologies that fight to win our hearts, minds, and actions?

## The Alternative: A Theology of Reconciliation

The alternative to these incomplete theologies is a theology based on God's character of reconciliation. Second Corinthians 5:18–19 says, "All this is from God, who reconciled us to himself through Christ and gave us the ministry of reconciliation: that God was reconciling the world to himself in Christ, not counting men's sins against them. And he has committed to us the message of reconciliation." To reconcile people to God and then to each other is the purpose of the gospel. This is the theology that is the true work of the church. If its structures and theologies cannot reconcile Jew and Gentile, slave and free, then we should question the church's validity as the representative of Jesus Christ. Maybe it is representing our own weaknesses and misrepresenting a gospel with the power of God to reconcile. "For we were all baptized by one Spirit into one body—whether Jews or Greeks, slave or free—and we were all given the one Spirit to drink" (1 Cor. 12:13).

We can begin to understand this alternative theology of reconciliation by defining the church. The church, as we all know, is the Body of Christ. It is the assembly of believers called out by God to be his people. These people see themselves as the replacements, the agents, for Jesus of Nazareth here on earth, in their own neighborhoods and communities. They are committed to being those agents in a specific neighborhood, in a return to the parish concept. Christian community development, then, is a return to the function God intended for the church, to be his replacement, his pinch hitter. This is a church that insists through its words and its actions that dehumanization in every form is blasphemy against God. We, the people of God, are called to live out our lives in our parishes in a way that reveals and affirms the dignity of those dehumanized by society.

Instead, we have turned the church into an institution that serves us instead of God. In fact, the church that we are most committed to is the church that will meet most of our personal and family needs. It has become popular for both black and white Christians to shop around for a church just as we shop around for food or clothing, and then join the one that offers the most "stuff." But our institutions are valuable in God's eyes only when they put flesh on the gospel. The gospel then becomes the love of God made visible, able to be touched and felt through physical agents of his kingdom. Only then is the gospel the good news to the poor that Jesus proclaimed. Living out the gospel means bringing the good news of God's love to people who are in need, demonstrating to them the love of Jesus and introducing them to the eternal life found only in him.

When I refer to eternal life I don't only mean the hereafter, but eternal life that begins here on earth and continues after. Jesus came to bring life, but also a certain quality of life. Jesus said, "I came that they may have life, and have it abundantly." Our task, then, is to enable people to have the abundant life that God desires for them. Abundant life surely begins with salvation, but it also includes having basic needs met and dignity affirmed.

In short, living the gospel means desiring for your neighbor and your neighbor's family that which you desire for yourself and your family. Living the gospel means bettering the quality of other people's lives—spiritually, physically, socially, and emotionally—as you better your own. Human beings have basic needs in all of these areas, and no institution should be as capable of meeting them as holistically as the church.

This is because the church's motivations are pure. We are motivated by love that is healthy as opposed to guilt that does only enough to ease the guilty feeling, or selfish ambition that does more to satisfy the helper than the helped. Therefore, we must ask ourselves two questions: What is the source of our motives? And what are the marks of an authentic church that is responding to the needs of our neighbors?

## The Attributes of an Authentic Church

There are seven attributes that we as the Body of Christ should be constantly trying to incorporate into our being.

*The authentic church absorbs pain.* The Old Testament foretold Jesus as one who would bear our suffering and our punishment (Isa. 52). At the synagogue, Jesus explained his mission as one of bringing good news to the poor and the suffering (Luke 4). He also says, "Come to me, all you who are weary and burdened, and I will give you rest" (Matt. 11:28). The church, as the agent of Jesus, should be a community in which pain and suffering can be brought to rest. An institution cannot do this; only a community can.

Our mission is to open our doors and invite pain and suffering in; Jesus did not absorb pain from a distance and neither can the church. This is a particularly important lesson for any congregation that wants to take its mission seriously. The urban poor are as acquainted with grief as any other people. The church should make every attempt to be a companion of and a comfort for this pain.

Until recently, the African-American church, for the most part, has played the role of comforter. The church house was where people went to find strength and encouragement in a discouraging and hostile environment. Church was where crushed and broken people, beaten down (sometimes literally) by an unsympathetic world, gathered to comfort each other and be comforted by worship and praise. It was where we rejoiced and looked to a heavenly future without the pain and suffering that we had grown accustomed to in the present.

Out of the church's responding to the needs of its suffering people came creativity, community, and a vital witness to the reality of the love of God. Today's prosperity theology, which says that if we follow God and do what's right we will rarely have pain or trouble, has drained this creativity and vitality from the church. If living for God is not a challenge, not a struggle, not a risk, if it does not require giving of one's self, then it becomes stagnant and lifeless.

*The authentic community of believers is also called to proclaim hope in a despairing world.* If we claim that the gospel offers hope to the world, we must be able to flesh out a living witness to that reality. Many inner-city workers discover that the gospel experience of their suburban church is not strong enough to sustain them in the despairing environment of inner-city pain. They discover that to demonstrate hope, they need the comfort and security, the hands, feet, and arms of an intentional community of believers with their same commitment to the city. The gospel works inside relationships, and it speaks from within concrete circumstances. The church lives out its call most fully when it is a community of faith with arms wrapped about a community of pain.

Leon Sullivan is the recently retired long-time pastor of Zion Baptist Church in Philadelphia. He was one of the developers of the Opportunities Industrialization Center, a job training and development center. He also developed the Sullivan Plan, a plan to use business as leverage to bring about justice and reconciliation in South Africa. (He abandoned this plan only a few years ago out of a belief that economic pressure alone could not bring about justice.) Leon to me is a real hero, one who has committed his life to proclaiming hope and making that hope real through action.

Leon, like me, came out of a broken home and was reared by his grandmother until he was in high school. He then went to West Virginia State College, a black college, on an athletic scholarship. Being at a black college developed his social conscience and sense of responsibility for his people. In his book *Build, Brother, Build* he describes how he heard the call to become a minister. He was in his sophomore year of college at the time:

> One day . . . I received a message that my grandmother was gravely ill, and I hurried to Charleston to see her. It was night when I arrived at the little wooden row house where she lived at that time. . . . As I looked about her room that night, I saw the misery of poverty. I noticed the wallpaper that had been plastered up layer over layer, thick and ragged, torn and spotted and damp. I noticed the pictures on the

wall that were covering holes, trying to decorate the place. . . . And as I sat there in the faint light of the oil lamp, amidst the dreariness and the smell of death, [my grandmother] looked up at me and said: "Leonie, help your people. And don't let this kind of thing happen to anybody else." The next Sunday I spoke to a group of young people in a church in Huntington, West Virginia, where I had gained some reputation as a speaker and leader. Standing there in that pulpit, I remembered what my grandmother had said, and somehow, inside, I knew what I must do and what I must be. I knew that I must be a minister of God, to work for Him, to help people who were poor, people who were in the kind of condition [my grandmother] was in. That Sunday afternoon my mission began; I had made my decision.[3]

Leon had committed himself to proclaiming hope to the poor in a very practical way: by working to change the conditions that produced their despair. His subsequent career fulfilled that commitment.

*An authentic church should point to God's authority.* All sorts of earthly powers claim the bodies and souls of the urban poor—from pimps and pushers and welfare to cults, television, and materialism. We, the community of believers, should demonstrate that we will not bend to destructive power because we obey an authority that rules over all other authorities. Our allegiance is to the righteous and just demands of our sovereign God, and no earthly power should control or intimidate us.

More than that, we encourage and enable others to become free of the earthly powers that destroy their lives. The courage to oppose the destructive powers of the world and the devil comes from the support of the community of faith. By proclaiming the sovereign authority of our just God, the church challenges and warns those who exploit the poor. The testimony of our life as a community, planted in the places of pain, should be our battle cry: "We intend by God's grace to chase away the demons of darkness." Says Orlando Costas: "[The church] is the community of believers that announces the Kingdom of God as a reality, which proclaims a new order of life under the sovereign action of God, which relativizes all human authority, including that of institutions."[4]

But we do not become proud and arrogant from proclaiming this. Rather, we experience what the disciples experienced after meeting with the resurrected Christ. They understood then that the kingdom of God has authority even over earthly powers; the final words they heard from their Master were: "*All authority* in heaven and on earth has been given to me. Therefore go" (Matt. 28:18–19, italics mine). They went and all eleven humbly carried the authority of Jesus. Historians still marvel at the rapid crumbling of the Roman Empire only decades after the disciples began their mission.

*The authentic church brings people together:* female and male, Jew and Samaritan, slave and free, black and white, Latino and Asian, suburbanite and ghetto dweller. God intended the church, the community of believers, to reconcile people to each other, beginning with the Jews. God called Abraham to be a blessing to all nations. God designed the temple to have a courtyard around it where all nations could gather to worship him. This meant that the Israelites had to pass among the members of several nations on their way to worship. When Christ was crucified, God tore open not only the veil of the Most Holy Place but also the wall separating the Courtyard of the Gentiles from the worship place of the Jews. No longer were the nations to be separated.

But the Israelites never understood this fundamental goal of their Lord. They confused God's choice of them as his special instrument of grace with God's favoritism. Their prejudice against other nations was evident throughout their history; they ignored God's call to make room for the alien and the stranger, to be instruments of healing for all the nations. When Jesus cleared the money changers from the courtyard, he told them they had turned the "house of prayer for all nations" (Mark 11:17) into a den of thieves and robbers. They were literally stealing from the world.

Today's church has similarly ignored God's call to be a blessing to all nations. Jesus said that when he was lifted up on the cross, all people would be drawn to him. All believers are to be united at the foot of the cross, demonstrating the power of God to reconcile people across divisions. Today, racism and factionalism are ripping the seams of our society. Violence has become the expression of the pain of our broken people; and the church, rather than seizing this opportunity to display God's reconciling power, has withdrawn and given its tacit approval to violence and division. This is nothing less than blasphemy against the Body of Christ; we have substituted racial and class separation for the reconciling love of God.

Today Christians study the science of withdrawing from others and then use it to attract converts. This so-called church growth or homogeneous principle should make us question the church the same way we should question dehumanizing ghettos. It sugarcoats racial separation with a veneer of spirituality and in practice continues the legacy of segregation that divided whites and blacks into separate churches, relationships, and agendas.

Homogeneity does not mirror the image of God. It cheapens the people who proclaim it and mocks God's call for us to be agents of reconciliation. What makes it even more harmful is how it is justified: "If we are segregated, more people will come and hear the gospel, which in turn, advances the kingdom of God." This logic spits in the face of a holy God by playing to our human weaknesses and sin nature. At the same time that it increases the size of our churches' membership, it retards their spiritual growth.

During the 1970s, I was on the steering committee to bring Billy Graham to Jackson, Mississippi. At that time our little church was the only one that I knew of in our city where blacks and whites worshiped together. In fact, one of our black members had tried to attend one of the larger white churches for a special Sunday evening service but was asked to leave because his presence was "disturbing the service." Although I agreed with the evangelical nature of the crusade, I also felt deep in my heart that the Christianity that could allow the behavior of the people at that church service was not truly representing the Jesus I had come to know and serve.

In order to make my feelings known to the steering committee I told them, "I am not sure that I want to be a part of making thousands more white Christians like the ones we already have in our city." Given my commitment to evangelism and my respect for Billy Graham, I did participate in the crusade. The crusade was a huge success; thousands of people accepted Christ. But it made very little difference in the hostile relationships between blacks and whites.

*The authentic church spends lavishly on the needy.* Think about this for a moment. When the community of faith assembles and takes an offering, God intends for this giving to benefit others, particularly the needy. Yahweh always told Israel to give abundantly of its resources to others; the New Testament church was instructed to follow this tradition, and Paul praised the Macedonian churches that gave "beyond" their ability. Jesus told the disciples that the widow who gave just a couple of mites gave more than the rich because she gave everything she had. Those who hold tightly onto their wealth find these teachings of Jesus very difficult. It's not surprising that Jesus said it is hard for a rich person to enter the kingdom. Robert Lupton describes this giving function of the church: "The church is the only institution which without irresponsibility, can expend all its resources on great and lavish outbursts of compassion. It is ordained to give itself away, yet without loss. The church, above all earthly symbols, bears the responsibility for declaring in the outpouring of resources, the utter dependability of God. To preserve its life is to lose it."[5]

Christians in relation to each other should care for each other so that none has to live in extreme need while others live in excess, and at the same time should do so in a way that affirms every person's dignity. We read about such a church community after Pentecost: "There were no needy persons among them. For from time to time those who owned lands or houses sold them, brought the money from the sales . . . and it was distributed to anyone as he had need" (Acts 4:34–35).

Today's church frequently spends only a fraction of its budget on others, devoting most of its offerings to itself, to buildings, or to internal activities. There are some remarkable exceptions. Some courageous churches have committed one-half or more of their offerings to meeting the needs of others. Some rural churches in the South also have a lesson to teach us. It is still a custom in some rural churches that when there is a need, an offering is taken and maybe even repeated several times until there is enough. Such churches often spend as much on those in need as on themselves—even when they themselves are by most middle-class American standards needy.

*The authentic church reflects God's character.* God's character has many aspects, such as compassion, gracious giving, and tenderness. We do not know which aspects of God's character are particularly needed in a community until we put ourselves there. Perhaps it will be courage and faith to persevere or love of enemies. Maybe it is the image of a father who is always there or an honest dealing with one's neighbor. We must realize that we cannot impose our understanding of God from the outside. It is only as we live in the community and find ourselves affected by the things that affect our neighbors that the character of God as we live it out becomes attractive to our neighbors. The message of Christ is not an irresistible aroma unless it is relevant to the needs of the people. When we demonstrate the character of God in dealing with situations that our neighbors are also faced with, and particularly in our relationships with them, then the gospel is made visible.

*The authentic community of faith protects the vulnerable.* I am amazed at the number of Christian leaders who protest the fact that God has a special concern for the downtrodden. Some Christian leaders insist that God is "no respecter" of persons, that he does not see anyone—including the poor—as deserving of more careful treatment than others.

There is probably no clearer theme in Scripture than God's concern for the fatherless, widows, and orphans—the most powerless in ancient societies—and God's command that his people care for the defenseless. In fact, along with worshiping false gods, God's most terrible wrath is reserved for people who have either ignored the plight of the poor or who have oppressed the poor. Look at the message of the prophets, such as Isaiah, who said, "Declare to my people their rebellion and to the house of Jacob their sins. . . . Is not this the kind of fasting I have chosen: to loose the chains of injustice and untie the cords of the yoke, to set the oppressed free and break every yoke?" (Isa. 58:1, 6). The urban poor, particularly the children, are America's chained and powerless.

When two patients come to an emergency room, a woman crushed by a runaway vehicle and a man who caught his finger in the medicine cabinet, a doctor mobilizes the hospital's most expert and well-trained staff to apply all their combined skills to save the life of the woman and nurture her toward full health. A nurse practitioner gives some codeine-enriched Tylenol and a bandage to the man and sends him home. More attention, resources, and care are given to the person in the greatest need.

Jesus was mocked for a life-style that kept him in the company of the vulnerable. Jesus loved the rich, but he always called them to a "richer" quality of life, which included a relationship with the poor. Zaccheus, the wealthy tax collector, exclaimed after his encounter with Jesus, "Here and now I give half of my possessions to the poor. . . ." (Luke 19:8). Recall the rich young ruler, whom Jesus calls to come and join his band of disciples, but first to "give all you have to the poor"(see Mark 10:21). True religion, the apostle James tells us, looks after the orphan and the widow.

Today's mainstream church, rather than protecting the powerless, has generally sold out to the powerful. We say that we want to have a "Christian influence" on the powerful, but to have that influence, we avoid doing or saying anything that might offend them. The powerful are influencing the church rather than the other way around when we allow the fear of being offensive to silence us.

I have served on the board of directors of many major Christian institutions in our nation. When we have tried to make a justice statement, these institutional leaders have found it very hard to make a clear statement on what constitutes justice. The reason for this is that when people have benefited from an unjust society it becomes very difficult for these same people to speak clearly on justice. Another example is the Arab-Israeli issue. True Christianity should call us to an evenhanded treatment of both Jews and Arabs. We ought to love and support both, but American evangelicals find it very, very hard to support the Arabs.

I believe that nothing other than the community of God's people is capable of affirming the dignity of the urban poor and enabling them to meet their own needs. Government has tried and most of its programs have failed. Private enterprise and parachurch organizations have taken on the role of the church and have played an important part in ministering to the urban poor. Many health care centers, drug rehabilitation programs, job training youth programs, and so on are often done best by people who can devote all their time and energy to these tasks in parachurch organizations.

The parachurch in America has developed many excellent programs, and I am very thankful for the work of many parachurch community development ministries. However, a Christian witness in the inner city (or anywhere), whether through a parachurch or a business enterprise, must be rooted in a worshiping fellowship of believers in a local church.

Circle Urban Ministries in inner-city Chicago drifted for seven years without a local church partner. Beneath the surface of successful ministry programs, says Circle director Glen Kehrein, "I suspected that our approach just might be more of a one-sided social gospel than I cared to admit." It wasn't until black pastor Raleigh Washington came on the scene to establish Rock of Our Salvation Evangelical Free Church and Raleigh and Glen teamed Rock and Circle up together that Circle really began changing lives.

Glen Kehrein has come to believe that "it's practically impossible for us, or anybody else, to do effective holistic ministry apart from the church. Circle has eighty people on staff and operates ten programs, such as housing, legal aid, medical, and education. Rock Church does the things churches normally do—evangelism, discipling, worship, youth programs, Christian education. Together, that's holistic ministry. The church has broadened our vision and made it possible for us to do together what neither of us could do separately. And we need the church for personal support. Without it, we couldn't survive."

As Glen has learned at the front lines of ministry, only relationships within the community of the local church can most fully:

> absorb pain
> proclaim hope
> point to God's authority
> bring people together
> spend lavishly
> reflect God's character
> protect the vulnerable

What could be more rewarding than living in such a family? We Christians have the tremendous privilege and opportunity of being called to such a life. And a broken and hurting world is waiting to see, to hear, to receive, and to be comforted.

# PART TWO

# OUR GOSPEL

# 4

# THE LIVING GOSPEL

Mary Nelson returned from the mission field of Africa and came face to face with racial unrest in Chicago. The neighborhood she moved into, West Garfield Park, had been devastated by the white flight of the 1960s and the cataclysmic disinvestment of the 1970s. The local Lutheran church, pastored by Mary's brother, was slowly losing its members to white flight.

Mary and her brother refused to leave, deciding instead to embrace the new community that had grown up around their church. Embracing these neighbors, however, was somewhat different than embracing their constituents of the past. The needs were different now. Better housing, better education, health care, and jobs were just a few of the areas that needed to be addressed if they were going to holistically witness and minister to this new community.

Today Bethel New Life, their Christian community development corporation, has renovated over five hundred units of housing, gives quality education to neighborhood children through its Christian school, provides quality health care for over eight hundred patients per month through its holistic health center, and directly and indirectly employs over five hundred neighborhood people through various small business ventures.

Mary Nelson is a living example of a woman who has allowed the incarnated love of Christ to move her to action. In allowing God to pour his love through her to the people in West Garfield Park, Mary embodies the powerful truth that the gospel is simply good news.

The gospel is the visible demonstration of the love of God. It is the manifestation of God's love in the world. This love is freely offered to us. The death of Christ on the cross was the ultimate way that God showed his love for us. Now we who believe in God have the wonderful task of manifesting God's love to the world. We are the agents through whom God demonstrates this love today.

From this understanding, we see that the gospel, the love of God, is about incarnation and transformation. God's ultimate demonstration of his love was through the incarnation of Christ: "The Word became flesh and made his dwelling among us. We have seen his glory, the glory of the One and Only, who came from the Father full of grace and truth" (John 1:14). Jesus Christ came to us, lived among us, and died for us. It was by knowing Jesus, God in man, that the disciples were able to know God: "He who has seen Me has seen the Father"(John 14:9 NASB). Today, God is incarnated in us, those who believe in him. We are the hands and feet of Christ in the world.

## Transformed by His Love

To carry out God's work, we must allow ourselves to be transformed by his love. Being transformed is a process that takes our entire lives, and we must remember that; we must bear in mind that we will not be perfected all at once. The process does, however, have a beginning point, at which we agree to allow God to work in our lives and to change us into the likeness of his Son. Until the process of transformation begins in us, we cannot love others as we must to demonstrate God's love to them. And unless we ourselves have experienced the transforming love of God personally, we cannot expect God's love to transform others.

So let me first talk about transformation. We are transformed as we are made aware, as we discover, God's love for us. Jesus told his followers, "The kingdom of heaven is like treasure hidden in a field. When a man found it, he hid it again, and then in his joy went and sold all he had and bought that field. Again, the kingdom of heaven is like a merchant looking for fine pearls. When he found one of great value, he went away and sold everything he had and bought it" (Matt. 13:44–46).

This parable tells us to cherish the kingdom of God above all else: "Seek ye first the kingdom of God, and his righteousness"(Matt. 6:33 KJV). Now, the love of God is bringing about the kingdom, is making us into the kingdom, as it reconciles us to God and to each other, as it motivates and enables us to do God's will. "Thy kingdom come, Thy will be done in earth, as it is in heaven" (Matt. 6:10 KJV). In order to cherish the kingdom, then, we need to cherish the gospel, the demonstration of the love of God, the same way.

When I first encountered the love of God, I treasured it because I had longed for love all of my life. I grew up without a mother and without a father. I grew up without the certainty of love in my life. I ached to be loved. Then, in a little Holiness mission in Pasadena, California, over thirty-five years ago, I heard Galatians 2:20 (KJV), "I have been crucified with Christ: nevertheless I live; yet not I, but Christ liveth in me: and the life which I now live in the flesh I live by the faith of the Son of God, *who loved me, and gave himself for me*" (italics mine). When I heard that God loved me enough to give himself in his Son for me, I reached out for that love. I wanted that certainty of love.

As I understood more of God's love for me, and the extremity of the sacrifice he made for me, I began to be transformed, little by little. I was overpowered by God's love that morning, and I wanted to share it with those whom I was coming in contact with. And as the love of God worked in my life, it was changing me so that God could use my life to demonstrate his love for others—and he is still at work in me today.

You see, when we accept the love of God, we allow the living Spirit of God to inhabit us. Because the Spirit is alive, every aspect of the way we live will be reshaped according to the new life that is inside us. The Spirit challenges our old ways of thinking, reshapes our directions and goals for our lives, rearranges our priorities, softens our hearts and makes them responsive to human pain and suffering, and replaces our selfishness with love for others. We are gradually made an incarnation of the love of God.

If we do not value the love of God above all other things, we will not give ourselves completely to it. If our families, our friends, our material wealth, our reputations, our worldly success, our physical lives are more important to us than the love of God, we will not benefit from all it offers us. If we reduce it to an idea that we agree with rather than an indwelling, living reality, we will gain only what an idea can give us. We will not allow the love of God to transform us, and we certainly will not expect it to transform anyone or anything else.

As we see the love of God at work transforming us, we come to understand that it can transform other people. We will begin to see that it can transform not only individual people, but groups of people, whole communities, institutions, societies. We also come to understand that God wants his transforming love to be at work in everyone everywhere. We are motivated even further to incarnate this love that dwells in us.

When I say that the love of God is an incarnated love, I mean that it is a love that expresses itself where there is need, not at a distance. Jesus came to show God's love to us—he did not demand that we come up to heaven to meet him—and so the love of God is most fully expressed where there is pain and suffering. If we as a community of Christians try to take the love of God to people who are hurting, we will discover, as Paul wrote, that the gospel is able to do far beyond what we think or ask. As a community, we become the expression of the living love of God. We are no longer just a group of people, but the incarnation of God's love. We are not "going to church"; we *are* the church.

Two of my children are part of an interracial Christian community in the inner city of Jackson, Mississippi. They call themselves "Antioch" after the first multiracial fellowship in the New Testament. Theirs and two other families covenanted together in 1986 to share their lives by buying a house and living in it together, welcoming others who are seeking spiritual development to live with them. Usually every room of their ten-bedroom, six-bath house is filled with people seeking direction, including single mothers, ex-offenders, and numerous teenagers. The life-style of the people at Antioch is to me what it truly means to be the church, to invite others to be deeply involved in our lives and our families.

When we recognize that the love of God is an incarnated love, we learn some important things about how this love acts in the world.

First of all, the love of God expresses itself in a specific place to meet the specific needs of specific people. It does not exist in an abstract theological vacuum. Orlando Costas writes that "[The gospel] is a witness that takes place in a given social and historical context. It is part of a living space with its own cultural, geographic, economic, social, and political characteristics, and it is carried out in a temporal moment, be it a generation or an epoch."[1] The work of the incarnate love of God in the world, then, is relevant. It affects people or societies in the circumstances within which they live. God listens to the cries of this world, and out of his depths of compassion, as shown to us in Christ's death on the cross, moves us, the people in whom he incarnates his love, to dry tears, heal wounds, set prisoners free, and break the yokes of oppression. That is why Christian community development insists that people locate themselves in the community of pain they desire to impact with the love of God. Otherwise, Costas writes, "Lack of a good understanding of the real issues involved in living in a particular situation will be reflected in inadequate or misdirected questions, and this will hinder our understanding of the relevance of the biblical message to that situation."[2]

We also learn that the gospel is made real to people by its effects, by the actions of the people who profess it. Anyone can offer a theory of salvation; hundreds of different cults have hundreds of different theories. The love of God, however, demonstrates its nature to us through the actions of its followers in society. The first Christians learned of the love of God by seeing Jesus in action in their lives. As the apostle John writes, "That which was from the beginning, which we have heard, which we have seen with our eyes, which we have looked at and our hands have touched—this we proclaim concerning the Word of life" (1 John 1:1). This, too, is related to transformation. One reason that the expression of the love of God is so often limited in Western society is that we do not expect it to change society and people except in a very spiritualized and narrowly defined way. We see the gospel as primarily rescuing us from hell and getting us to heaven. We have lost sight of "Thy kingdom come, Thy will be done in earth as it is in heaven." And when we do not expect it to change lives, we will not see it change lives.

If the love of God is to become more real to us, we must put ourselves in a place where believers are asking God to incarnate his love in them in order to address the needs around them. Then we can watch his love transform not only the people around us but ourselves as well because God will require that we be part of the work of the gospel. He will stretch us to the limits of our ability to love and then show us that his love, which is far greater than ours, can enter into us.

There are many Christians whose response to the love of an indwelling Christ has compelled them to pass on that love to their neighbors, but often that has not been accomplished without extreme personal sacrifice. At our 1990 Christian Community Development Association (CCDA) annual convention, Mary Nelson shared with us some of the painful experiences that would have devastated and chased away people whose actions were motivated by personal gain or guilt, and not by a love for God. One of Mary's most painful stories was of a brutal physical attack and rape that left her nearly dead.

It would have been easy to become alienated from her community after this experience. Instead, through God's grace in the midst of her pain, Mary became more determined to create a safe, healthy community for herself and her neighbors. Now, years later, Mary can say, "I believe we're just about to the point where we're going to tip this neighborhood for the positive. On the corridor where we've focused our greatest efforts you see flowers, picket fences, green gardens—like the suburbs. In a year, we probably touch ten thousand of the forty thousand people in our community." Mary's hope and undying positive spirit flow out of the love that she has experienced from God, even in the midst of personal pain.

Finally, we learn that even though the incarnate love of God is present with us, its incarnation is ultimately a mystery to us. We have to remember that it comes out of God's reaching out to us, not the other way around. We must remember that we cannot fully understand the incredible goodness of God, who loved us enough to die for us. We have to remain reverent and in awe before the power of God's love to transform lives. We must remember that as God uses us to do his work, it is his power at work in us, which is not limited by our human limitations. "But we have this treasure in jars of clay to show that this all-surpassing power is from God and not from us" (2 Cor. 4:7). So we must be humble about our understanding of the love of God.

We must keep this humility as we approach the communities of need in which God incarnates his love through us. If we do not wish to learn about the mystery of God's love for us from the people of those communities, we will never be able to minister effectively there. If we assume we already know what the love of God looks like or how it is expressed, we will overlook the ways it is already there and be unable to show that love to the people. We need to be willing to let God teach us, encourage us, and reveal his love to us anew from the people we want to serve.

So God calls us to be transformed by his love in order to make us instruments of his love to the whole world. Who could ask for a greater privilege? Who could imagine a more exciting and joyful calling? Let us ask God to help us treasure his love enough that it can transform us; to give us the grace to put ourselves in a place where we can meet specific needs of specific people; to help us always remember that our actions, not only our words, are the demonstration of the truth of his love; and to keep us humble about our understanding of his love and grateful that he is at work in us.

# 5

# THE BURDEN OF PROOF

The authentic demonstration of the gospel is a way of life that turns the values and the agenda of society upside down. One way the Christian life-style is called to contradict the world is in our love for the poor. Upward mobility is society's rule for success, and even those who grew up in the inner city get as far away as they can from the poor. But because of God's special concern for the poor and oppressed, our closeness to them is a reliable test of our authenticity. Jesus not only lived and moved among the poor, but at crucial times in his ministry he pointed to his love for the poor as the proof of his lordship.

One such moment was when John the Baptist was in prison, knowing that his life might end at any time. It was a time of struggle for him, and a troubling question plagued him: Was Jesus really the promised One, the Messiah? The meaning of John's life hinged on the answer. Was there a purpose for the pain of prison or had he given himself to a worthless cause?

John sent his disciples to Jesus, bringing with them John's desperate question. "Art thou he that should come," they asked Jesus, "or do we look for another?"(Matt. 11:3 KJV). John needed a conclusive sign, a message that would authenticate Jesus, so that he could die in peace, confident that he had prepared the way and had announced the Messiah in keeping with the Old Testament prophecies.

How did Jesus answer? The Bible says, "In that same hour he cured many of their infirmities and plagues, and of evil spirits; and unto many that were blind he gave sight. Then Jesus answering, said unto them, Go your way, and tell John what things ye have seen and heard; how the blind see, the lame walk, the lepers are cleansed, the deaf hear, the dead are raised, to the poor the gospel is preached" (Luke 7:21–22 KJV).

When John's disciples asked Jesus who he was, the burden of proof was on him to provide the answer. Jesus did not answer John's question with mere words; he authenticated his messianic claim by his actions. In fact, his deeds that followed—healing the blind and lame and lepers and preaching good news to the poor—were in fulfillment of the prophecy in Isaiah 61 concerning the Messiah and the favorable year of the Lord.

This same Scripture was the basis for Jesus' "inaugural address," his first public sermon in which he announced himself and his mission to the Jews: "The Spirit of the Lord is on me, because he has anointed me to preach good news to the poor. He has sent me to proclaim freedom for the prisoners and recovery of sight for the blind, to release the oppressed, to proclaim the year of the Lord's favor" (Luke 4:18–19).

As Jesus sent John's disciples away, echoing the prophecy of Isaiah 61 once again (Luke 7:22–23), they knew exactly what he was saying, even though he never gave a straight-out "yes." Jesus' actions in answer to John's question recalled the Old Testament prophecy about the ministry of the Messiah. Among the poor, Jesus authenticated his claim to be the Son of God. John's disciples returned to his prison cell as eyewitnesses of the proof of Jesus' lordship. Now, no matter what happened to him, John could die in peace. He had fulfilled his task; he had prepared the way for the Messiah.

## Demonstrating Our Authenticity

Today, the burden of proof is on the church of Jesus Christ, the people of God. As the old Prince Albert ad used to say, "The proof is in the puffing." How is an unbelieving world to know who the real people of God are? We must demonstrate that we are the people of God by our actions, by our concern for the poor and the oppressed of our society. We must remove society's blinders and replace them with a Christ-like compassion for the poor. Without this manifestation of our faith, without this "proof," then our proclamation of it is hollow.

The apostle James says, "Suppose a brother or sister is without clothes and daily food. If one of you says to him, 'Go, I wish you well; keep warm and well fed,' but does nothing about his physical needs, what good is it? In the same way, faith by itself, if it is not accompanied by action, is dead" (James 2:15–17). The apostle John says, "Dear children, let us not love with words or tongue but with actions and in truth. This then is how we know that we belong to the truth, and how we set our hearts at rest in his presence" (1 John 3:18–19). It is our very life-style, in imitation of Jesus, that becomes, like Jesus, a stumbling block to those who teach a way of life that denounces the nature of the kingdom.

There are many ways that we Christians might demonstrate our authenticity to society. Society would say that marriages cannot survive twentieth-century values. Our healthy marriages demonstrate that we disagree. Society would say that babies in the womb have to be sacrificed for convenience or for escaping economic hardship. Our care for pregnant women (especially single ones), our making available adoption services and job training, and our stand against abortion demonstrate that we disagree. Society would say that ethnic groups cannot live in harmony. Our deep and trusting interracial relationships and our thriving multiracial churches demonstrate that we disagree. Society says that inevitably there must be the haves and the have-nots. Our church life that defies socioeconomic traditions demonstrates that we disagree.

Historically, however, what we the church do has not matched up with what we say. When I speak in suburban churches, both white and black, and call for an inner city life-style that will demonstrate the gospel to the poor, I am not asking for something that is easy. It is very difficult because many suburban churches do not disciple people who are capable of answering such a call. In many cases their discipleship goes only as far as their suburban life-style will let it. Then they make the mistake of organizing their Christianity around their chosen life-style, rather than vice versa.

We who claim to be biblically conservative must deal honestly with the fact that the demonstration of the gospel in our corporate church life does not measure up with our claim to have the power of the gospel and the presence of God in our midst. Howard Snyder says, "When we speak of such matters as class divisions, racial discrimination, institutionalism, neglect of the poor and the inner city, and lack of social conscience and cultural impact, we are confronting problems that are just as present (and sometimes more so) in evangelical and fundamentalist churches as in the so-called liberal churches."[1]

When Jesus confronted the Pharisees because their religious life-style did not demonstrate the substance of the law, he was not having a doctrinal argument. His point to them was that they tithed and kept the Sabbath, yet neglected the "more important matters of the law," which was to do "justice, mercy and faithfulness"(Matt. 23:23). They had taken care to follow every legalistic requirement of the law but had missed the main point of their faith. Jesus came up with all sorts of names for them because they distorted God's message: whitewashed tombs, brood of vipers, hypocrites, and others. We, too, are tempted to go the way of society by ignoring the more important matters of the law and neglecting those who are poor and crushed in spirit.

## Connecting Words and Deeds

Jim Wallis's classic book *Agenda for Biblical People* suggests that Christ's life-style of caring for the needy was in fact calling for a "new order" that is "at odds with the values of the world."[2] He continues:

> The apostle James well described the difference between living faith and empty faith. Dead faith bears no fruit, shows no evidence of transformation. The criterion to judge faith is the quality of the believer's life as a living witness [demonstration] to the Gospel, not mere assent to doctrine and creed. In the Gospel of Luke, Jesus rebukes those who call him Lord but fail to demonstrate obedience: "Why do you call me 'Lord, Lord' and do not what I tell you?"[3]

Wallis goes on to describe the passage in Matthew 25 where many will assemble before God who all their lives had referred to him as "Lord." Jesus will tell them that he does not recognize them, that he never knew them, and that he will condemn them to hell. He then makes the basis of his judgment very plain:

> I was hungry and you gave me nothing to eat,
> I was thirsty and you gave me nothing to drink,
> I was a stranger and you did not invite me in,
> I needed clothes and you did not clothe me,
> I was sick and in prison and you did not look after me.
>                                                    [Matt. 25:42–43]

We make a serious error if we ignore these passages because of a lame doctrinal scheme that allows us to spiritualize them. I was in Houston doing a workshop when I encountered just this kind of spiritualizing perspective. As I went through the biblical foundations of Christian community development I gave my definition of the gospel, which is "the visible demonstration of God's love." A pastor in the back of the room raised his hand at this point and said, "I disagree with your definition of the gospel." The definition of the gospel, he said, is found in 1 Corinthians 15:1–5 where Paul says, "I want to remind you of the gospel I preached to you. . . . By this gospel you are saved, if you hold firmly to the word I preached to you . . . that Christ died for our sins according to the Scriptures, that he was buried, that he was raised on the third day according to the Scriptures, and that he appeared to Peter, and then to the Twelve." He insisted that my definition required more of a believer than the Bible itself did, since the Bible to him said that all a person had to do in order to be saved was "hold firmly" to the gospel as it is presented in 1 Corinthians 15.

Another person spoke up and said that his grandmother was the sweetest woman in the whole world, that he was sure she was saved and going to heaven, but that she had a tiny problem: She was racist against black people. "How can the love of God abide in you if you hate your brother?" I quoted from Scripture. She is still going to heaven, they insisted, even if she never stops hating black people, because she has believed the gospel.

This theology, which allows people to hate their neighbors while claiming to believe in the gospel, did not suddenly appear one day in Houston. You see, American theology developed during the time of slavery. The church had to come up with a theological justification so that it could continue to enjoy the benefits of slavery. Out of this came that warped theological perspective that separates what people say and believe from what they do. Lots of people during the time of slavery claimed to be Christians and yet hated "niggers."

It is an ironclad truth of our Christian faith that we are sinners who are saved by grace alone: "For it is by grace you have been saved, through faith—and this not from yourselves, it is the gift of God—not by works, so that no one can boast" (Eph. 2:8–9).

But I do not agree that Christians can separate what we believe from what we do. It has always baffled me why in discussing this we leave out the very next verse in that passage from Ephesians: "For we are God's workmanship, created in Christ Jesus to do good works, which God prepared in advance for us to do." Yes, we are saved by grace through faith but, according to this very next verse, we are saved to do good works. The works don't save us; yet if good works don't accompany our salvation, then how is the world to know that we are the people of God?

Works set true Christians apart from pretenders. Separating what we believe from what we do has greatly harmed our credibility as Christians and has left room for all sorts of religions, sects, hip hoppers, and filmmakers to vie for the hearts and souls of our urban youth. The urban subculture that has grown up around Malcolm X and groups like the Black Muslims are all evidence of our people's search for some truth to believe in. It is not necessary to replace Christianity with a new "gospel" or a clever distortion. But it *is* necessary that we begin to live out our faith to its fullest.

When our method or pattern of church life nurtures racism, sexism, avoidance of those in harsh conditions, deference to the wealthy, and quiet support of oppressive structures, then we have, in fact, demonstrated that the gospel does allow for these behaviors. We have agreed with the prince of this world. But Pastor William Jones reminds us, "Almost always [Jesus] referred to Himself as the Son of man. But the Church has presented Him in celestial colors and royal regalia which He did not request or desire. In stressing his divinity, the Church has nearly forgotten His humanity. . . . He lived among men before dying for men. . . . [On the cross] divine love expressed itself through the greatest human concern: 'Greater love hath no man than this, that a man lay down his life for his friends.'" [4]

Ultimately, we can say that the gospel is a physical event. The cross was a physical event. People stood there and witnessed the evidence of Christ's love. Love must be seen to be embraced. If we are unable to connect our words to our deeds then we have in fact not yet presented the gospel to society. Words have become not only a crutch but a lethal poison that deludes sour minds into thinking we are bearing witness to Christ because we have exercised our tongues.

It should not surprise us that all the great revivals and awakenings included the demonstration of the gospel. John Wesley, who led revivals in the nineteenth century, did more than just talk about social reform. Among other things, he agitated for prison, liquor, and labor reform; set up loan funds for the poor; campaigned against the slave trade and smuggling; opened a dispensary and gave medicines to the poor; worked to solve unemployment; and personally gave away considerable sums of money to people in need.[5]

In America, however, these revivals and awakenings were not all that remarkable because they were not strong enough to deal with the race issue. Our history books talk about the wonderful things that happened, but when the revivals and awakenings were over, the lives of us blacks had seen little significant improvement. When people say to me, "Let's go back to the religion of our founding fathers," I say to them, "I don't want to go back to that religion. I would still be a slave."

Our demonstration of God's love cannot be modeled after revivals that excluded people on the basis of race. Neither can it be modeled after the failure of the gospel in the urban community. When the neighborhoods began to deteriorate white Christians fled from our cities into the suburbs. Often our black congregations are more concerned with having a building than they are in creating a sense of community. The worst parts of our cities may have seven or eight churches on a block.

The various movements we have seen recently are not quite the model either. The evangelical movement found itself captured by the Moral Majority and the Republican party, but it finally failed. The charismatic movement grew rapidly but ended up being caught in the midst of immorality scandals. This movement, for the most part, did not have its anchor among the poor outside of exploiting them for donations. The signs and wonders movement has yet to authenticate itself among the poor. The prosperity movement is heavily accepted among the poor but has done very little in terms of real community development at the grass roots level. It takes people's attention away from the problem, and if those people succeed it encourages them to remove themselves from the very people they ought to be identifying with and working among.

## Facing the Crisis

We the church face a crisis in terms of the gospel we preach because we have not authenticated ourselves to the world around us. It amazes me how we can be so versed in the Scriptures yet never get around to asking ourselves the right questions. The burden of proof is on us just as it was on Jesus. When Jesus was asked by the disciples of John to give proof of his messianic claims, he did so by his actions. He said to go and tell John not only what they heard but also what they saw: "the blind see, the lame walk, the lepers are cleansed, the deaf hear, the dead are raised, to the poor the gospel is preached"(see Matt. 11:5). If we are to be Jesus' replacement on earth then we should constantly ask ourselves this same question: How do we as Christians demonstrate the proof of our claims to the world? If the church will ever authenticate its claim to be "the answer," "the way," "the good news," then we will prove that claim, as Jesus did, among the poor and oppressed.

# 6

# FILLING THE LEADERSHIP VACUUM

"It's not hard to create a ghetto," says Bob Lupton, Atlanta community developer. "Just remove the capable neighbors. To produce a substandard school system, withdraw the students of achieving parents. To create a culture of chronically dependent people, merely extract the upwardly mobile role models from the community.

"That's what happened in thousands of communities across the United States. That's what happens when we pursue our own personal and family dreams, and abandon our neighbors to the agencies."

There are many Americans who, like me, marched, demonstrated, and risked their lives so that African Americans would no longer have to remain in a "second-class" status and that all Americans would have equal access to the life, liberty, and pursuit of happiness we all cherish so much. To these committed people, the reality of today's urban blight leaves a bitter taste in the mouth.

There are many reasons for the development of this relatively new breed of poverty: government dependency; the legacy of racism; the moral and spiritual decay of which drugs, crime, and violence are a symptom; and, of course, disintegration of the family—all these things have contributed greatly to our urban problems.

There is also another subtle cause that ironically stems from the very success of our struggle for freedom. The success of the civil rights movement meant we no longer had to ride in the back of the bus. Success meant no longer attending inferior segregated schools. Then, after the Fair Housing Act passed in 1968, success also came to mean that we could live in whatever neighborhood we could afford.

Now some of us had a new option, and we seized it. Many of our best-trained minds—our moral, spiritual, and social leaders, the professionals, college and school teachers, and other upwardly mobile people previously forced to live in all-black neighborhoods, where maids and business owners alike lived on the same street—could now move up and out in search of a better life. These leaders had been the stabilizing glue that held our communities together. The exodus of their families, their skills, and their daily civic and moral leadership hastened the unraveling of the inner city, leaving a vacuum of leadership.

The central goal of Christian community development is to restore that stabilizing glue and fill the vacuum of moral, spiritual, and economic leadership that is so prevalent in poor communities.

There are two ways to accomplish this task, both of which are crucial to an effective Christian community development strategy. The first thrust is indigenous leadership development—raising up Christian leaders from the community of need who will remain in the community. The second thrust is for committed Christians and their families to live in communities of need, filling the leadership vacuum by modeling healthy life-styles.

## Indigenous Leadership Development

To believe in indigenous leadership development is to believe in the inherent dignity of the people who need developing. If you don't believe that they can eventually lead themselves then you must believe that they are somehow inferior to you. This type of attitude manifests itself in relationships that are patronizing, self-gratifying, and dependent. If there is one thing that America has learned it is that charity without development is unhealthy for both giver and receiver.

The ultimate affirmation is to say to a child, "I believe in you." Any oppressed people must believe that they can "drink from their own wells." This is the essence of indigenous leadership development: for the teacher to one day say, "I believe that you will some day become a leader," and to work diligently at making that day happen.

Leadership development is key to anyone's attempting to do effective ministry. Jesus said, "You did not choose me, but I chose you and appointed you to go and bear fruit—fruit that will last" (John 15:16). We have seen over the years that the key to bearing lasting fruit is not in developing programs. The key is in developing people—leaders. I believe that developing creative leaders is both the most essential and the most difficult part of Christian community development. It was the heart of Jesus' strategy. It must be the center of our strategy, too.

I returned to Mendenhall, Mississippi, from California in 1960 and saw the many problems my neighborhood faced. As we watched what was happening to our young people in that community, I said to my wife, Vera Mae, "If we are going to make a difference in this community, we must help these young people get a love for God, a love for themselves, and a love for their community—a love that is greater than consumerism and selfish materialism. We must help them stay in school and then go off to college and to get skills and education with a purpose. Then we must encourage those young people to bring those skills back to the community."

Twelve years later, Dolphus and Rosie Weary and Artis and Carolyn Fletcher and other young people began to come back to that neighborhood. Their fresh leadership allowed Vera Mae and me to move on to Mississippi's capital city of Jackson. There we worked for ten years doing the same thing. Today, a young man named Melvin Anderson, who grew up in the programs in both Mendenhall and Jackson, has taken over the reins of leadership.

After leadership was raised up in Jackson we moved on to Northwest Pasadena, California. We've been here eleven years and leadership is emerging again.

One of the reasons that developing leaders is so difficult is because it requires a long-term commitment. Only if you are willing to invest your life in the life of another for the long haul will you be effective in leadership development. We have found that an investment of ten to fifteen years is necessary.

## Modeling Healthy Life-styles

Another way of restoring the stabilizing glue to our urban areas is for committed Christians to live in these communities. The importance of our physical presence in these communities can't be overstated, whether it means moving to them for the first time, coming back, or just staying put. This principle that we have come to call *relocation* is what has given Christian community development success as well as undeniable credibility. Even before I gave it a name, many Christians across the country already knew it in their hearts and were already living it out. It is a concrete way to answer God's call for them to do ministry among the poor.

In October 1992 over seven hundred Christians representing over 150 churches and organizations came together in Detroit for the fourth annual Christian Community Development Association convention. This grass roots movement has been successful largely because its focus has remained clear: tough-minded Christians all across the country moving their families into or choosing to stay put in deteriorating communities and making a stand for Christ, saying that they will take responsibility for this community.

Like any movement that is exciting and making an impact, people from all walks of life will be drawn to it. They see the impact that the movement is making, they sense the excitement of the people, and they can feel the power of God at work. But as is true with many historical movements, in order to widen the appeal so that more people can get involved, there is pressure to water down the commitments needed to realize the vision.

There are many ways to do urban ministry and many of them are good. I cheer for anyone who is making a sincere attempt to show Christ's love to the poor—they have my deepest respect. But one of the distinguishing marks of Christian community development is its commitment to *living among the poor*. Because this commitment is sometimes dangerous—because it means making many specific sacrifices, because it means giving up many of the options accessible to middle-class Christians and tying your future and the future of your family in with the poor—many who want to be a part of the movement but are unwilling to make these sacrifices attack the *relocation* principle.

"Relocation does not have to be literal," said one young man. "As long as you relocate in your heart—that's what's important to God." That really sounds spiritual, but I'm glad that Jesus didn't just relocate in his heart. We can all be thankful that he came to earth in the flesh.

"If we focus too much on relocation," pleaded a suburban woman, "we run the risk of being elitist." I can hardly imagine it being elitist to move into some of our tough inner-city neighborhoods. When it becomes elitist, it will then be time to find another mission field.

It is very important that we remember what makes us who we are. A few years ago, a reporter was writing a story about Voice of Calvary Ministries in Mississippi. She said that she was trying to pinpoint the one thing that made that ministry unique. She finally concluded that it wasn't just the fact that the staff was doing a lot of good ministry in the target area, but they were living there, too. "You all live where you are ministering." That became the focus of her story.

Relocation is an ideal. There is no question that our ministry will be more effective if we are living among the people we serve. Certainly God is not calling everyone to live out the ideal. If he has something better for you to do, praise God. But even then, we should still be able to affirm the ideal and recognize that our efforts will only go as far as our commitment. Deep problems require sacrificial solutions. Let's not water down the ideal for those God *is* calling to relocate. For those who are called to do it, living among the poor is the best investment we can make.

## A Caution

The idea of hundreds of middle-class families moving back into the inner cities of this country should not be confused with gentrification. In many cities young, middle-class professionals are moving back into the cities, restoring old houses and apartment complexes and displacing the poor. Why make that long commute every day to the city? Why pay the outrageous prices for a house in the suburbs when you can get property for almost nothing in the inner city?

The difference between relocation and gentrification is motive, plain and simple. When we decide to move into an inner-city neighborhood we should always ask ourselves the question, *Is this good for my new neighbors?* Moving into inner-city neighborhoods for merely selfish reasons with no regard as to how it will affect the community residents will probably eventually do harm to your neighbors.

In most urban areas around the country (there are a few exceptions), there is room for hundreds of families to reclaim abandoned neighborhoods. The deteriorating Summerhill community of Atlanta once was home to more than twenty thousand residents. Today its numbers have dwindled to five thousand. Several thousand "good neighbors" could easily move into this old neighborhood without worry of displacing the people who still call Summerhill home. In fact, this is exactly what Bob Lupton and other Atlanta community activists are attempting to do.

Summerhill is strategically located at the future site of the 1996 summer Olympics. This has given concerned Atlanta residents extra motivation to turn this nearly abandoned neighborhood around. The strategy that Lupton is counting on to revive this once thriving community is relocation—hundreds of middle-class families moving into this neighborhood and breathing new life into it.

From L.A. to Philadelphia, Detroit to Dallas, even on Chicago's dreaded Westside, stable Christian families, motivated by their desire to participate in the rebuilding of our inner cities, are sprinkling back in, buying homes, setting down roots, and building relationships with unlikely neighbors. They are convinced that their presence is the surest way to begin tackling the problems of their cities.

Urban communities need our best and brightest. They need strong two-parent families. They need to see with their own eyes disciplined families with a strong work ethic and meaningful values. They need to experience families that are not only concerned about their own families, but who also take an active interest in children whose families are not so fortunate.

How many of us are called to make this type of sacrifice, I don't know. I do believe that many are called to make this type of commitment. One thing is sure: All of us are called to make some kind of response to the poor. Everyone has a role to play—even if God has not called you to move into a low-income neighborhood and live and work directly among the poor.

In the chapters that follow, I will be discussing many things we can do to make God's love visible among the poor. But focusing on the "how-to's" can easily distract us from what really matters most: our mission. We can be doing a lot of good things and miss the best or even look back after years of effort and see little real change in the lives of people.

A key question that we should be constantly asking ourselves when trying to hear God's voice is: *Where and how can I make the most impact on the lives of the poor?* For some the answer might be supporting those who are living in poor communities—by offering time and skills and by supporting them emotionally and financially. For many this will be the best contribution they can make. For others who hear the call on their lives clearly, relocation could be the means by which they will answer the call of God to minister to the poor. Either way, the mark of effectiveness will be—as it was for Jesus—leaving behind indigenous leaders who love God and love their neighbors.

# 7

## EVANGELISM

My son Derek was converted while he was in college at Jackson State. As he describes it, he made a "U-turn." His desire to serve God led him to begin working with a group of twelve-year-old boys, none of whom were Christians at the time. All of them were labeled by the school system as on their way to failure. They came from broken homes. They were at the bottom of society.

One of these boys, Kevin Adams, was a gang leader and a drug user at age twelve. He was violent; once Derek had to deal with his pulling a gun. When Derek began spending time with Kevin, Kevin's teacher told him, with Kevin present, "Kevin will never amount to anything. Don't waste your time with him. Just get him out of my classroom." Derek quickly took Kevin out of that negative classroom but ignored the rest of that teacher's advice.

Derek demonstrated his care for Kevin by spending time with him, helping him with his homework, taking him places, punishing him when he deserved it, and encouraging him to work to accomplish his dreams. As a result Kevin wanted to know more about the God whom Derek loved so much and who motivated Derek to love Kevin. Through Derek's holistic evangelism, Kevin became a Christian. Kevin also discovered that he liked math and began to earn good grades at his new school. He pursued his dream of being a carpenter by spending time with Derek's friends who were carpenters. He stopped fighting, got out of gangs, got off drugs. He became a leader among the group of boys; Derek could call on him to discipline the others.

When Vera Mae and I moved to Pasadena and started Harambee in 1982, Derek was with us. By this time his group of boys had become young adults, and a couple of them were Christian leaders in Jackson. We hadn't been on the corner of Howard and Navarro for too long before it became clear that we needed help in standing against the drug dealers. Derek called Kevin and asked him to come out and help. Kevin was on the next bus to Los Angeles. He was a crucial partner to Derek in our struggle against the drug dealers.

Although at times he still struggles, today Kevin is an accomplished carpenter and a devoted husband and father. Kevin is setting a much-needed example in a neighborhood that is like most ghetto neighborhoods, where very few young black men are married or working at legitimate jobs.

True evangelism, as in the lives of Derek and Kevin, dynamically impacts the lives of both the converted and those around them. What separates Christian community development from other forms of social change is that we believe that changing a life or changing a community is ultimately a spiritual issue. Evangelism and social responsibility are two sides of one coin. They are inseparable. Real evangelism calls us to see our sins for what they are. Then we turn to God in repentance and receive the forgiveness of sins. If we have received the forgiveness of sins, the gift of personal relationship with God, and the promise of everlasting life, then how can we not share such great news with others?

Unfortunately, often the debate over how to do evangelism becomes confused with the value of evangelism itself. I want to be clear that a ministry of Christian community development without evangelism is like a body without a soul. To be Christian, by definition, is to live and speak in such a way that our lives continually point to the wonderful person of Jesus.

I want to answer three questions in this chapter: Why evangelism? What is evangelism? What is the consequence of evangelism?

## Why Evangelism?

It is beyond human comprehension, but the human race was created for fellowship with God. God desires fellowship with his created human race in spite of our sinfulness. The first glimpse of this desire comes in the Garden of Eden, that first evening after Adam and Eve ate fruit that God had forbidden them to eat. God was not willing to end the relationship and sought them out even though they were avoiding him. When God called Abraham to follow him and promised to make the patriarch a great nation, God established that covenant in order to form relationships with humanity. Animal sacrifices to atone for sin were instituted to satisfy the need for justice. God intended Abraham and the nation of Israel to make it possible for all nations to worship him and to come into relationship with him, and this was the means that God provided at that time.

None of us can presume to understand why, centuries later, God chose to satisfy the requirements of justice through the blood of Jesus, removing once and for all the barrier to fellowship with him. The sacrifice of his Son was the costliest and most painful option to God. We see from that sacrifice how great God's love is for us, and we can be thankful that we are not required to restore relationship through Old Testament means. Now all men and women may have complete and restored relationship to God through the work of Jesus.

I do not need to repeat the work of many theologians in explaining the mystery of salvation through grace. My answer to the question of "why evangelism?" is consistent with the 1974 Lausanne Covenant. Christian community development includes the urgent need to bring all people into a saving relationship with Jesus. I fully agree with the third paragraph of the Covenant:

*The Uniqueness and Universality of Christ*

We affirm that there is only one Savior and one Gospel, although there is a wide diversity of evangelistic approaches. We recognize that all men have some knowledge of God through His general revelation in nature. But we deny that this can save, for men suppress the truth by their unrighteousness. We also reject as derogatory to Christ and the Gospel every kind of syncretism and dialogue which implies that

Christ speaks equally through all religions and ideologies. Jesus Christ, being Himself the only God-man, who gave Himself as the only ransom for sinners, is the only mediator between God and man. There is no other name by which we must be saved. All men are perishing because of sin, but God loves all men, not wishing that any should perish but that all should repent. Yet those who reject Christ repudiate the joy of salvation and condemn themselves to eternal separation from God. To proclaim Jesus as the "Savior of the World" is not to affirm that all men are either automatically or ultimately saved, still less to affirm that all religions offer salvation in Christ. Rather, it is to proclaim God's love for a world of sinners and to invite all men to respond to Him as Savior and Lord in the wholehearted, personal commitment of repentance and faith. Jesus Christ has been exalted above every other name; we long for the day when every knee shall bow to Him and every tongue shall confess Him as Lord.

Being in fellowship with God speaks both to our eternal condition and our present condition. Eternally, we cannot have fellowship with God without the saving work of Jesus. God desires our company forever, and the shed blood of Jesus allows us into that reward if we put our faith in the work of Calvary.

We cannot live in the present without the knowledge and power of that fellowship with God. We may "exist" but it is Christ who gives us "life." Without this fellowship, we are in bondage to the evil one. Our lives are controlled by the powers of darkness. We are literally being killed and destroyed. We need to be saved from this condition, and by some mystery the work of the Holy Spirit, which can transform us from children of the darkness to children of the light, will reverse the destruction we bring to ourselves.

So the reason for our evangelism is not only the good news that God desires and has established a means for us to have relationship with him. It is also the news that we can be saved from ourselves.

How could Derek, having received this treasure that transforms us into the likeness of our loving God, withhold it from the hurting boys who lived on his street? The love brought into our lives by the indwelling Spirit of God should move us to share this good news with all who have not heard. The passionate desire for others to share in this good news makes us into evangelists.

## What Is Evangelism?

An ugly debate has raged for the last seventy years over whether or not evangelism is the same as social action. This debate has its roots in truth: Each side has chosen one of these two essential aspects of the gospel, and neither is willing to consider its chosen part "optional."

Evangelicals doing community development need to come to terms with this debate and then move on to the work at hand. I want to be clear that there is no competition between evangelism and social responsibility. If I were to spend all my time teaching my children the Bible, but not lift a finger to see that they are fed, that they are educated, that they are job-prepared, that they learn to give to others, I could justly be called an irresponsible parent. In the same way, our love for others is questionable if either spiritual or social concern is lacking. Jesus never put evangelism and social action at odds with each other, so neither should we. All we should be asking is how they should be done.

I define evangelism as showing what God the Holy Spirit is doing in my life. It is answering the question, "What is God up to?" We should be living our lives in a way that will motivate others to become God-loving people. As we go about this life-style we will discover that we are proclaiming the good news of Jesus and that our presence and actions are essential to this proclamation. The fourth paragraph of the Lausanne Covenant states:

> To evangelize is to spread the Good News that Jesus died for our sins and was raised from the dead according to the Scriptures, and that as the reigning Lord He now offers the forgiveness of sins and the liberating gift of the Spirit to all who repent and believe. Our Christian presence in the world is indispensable to evangelism, and so is that kind of dialogue whose purpose is to listen sensitively in order to understand. But evangelism itself is the proclamation of the historical, Biblical Christ as Savior and Lord, with a view to persuading people to come to Him personally and so be reconciled to God. In issuing the Gospel invitation we have no liberty to conceal the cost of discipleship. Jesus still calls all who would follow Him to deny themselves, take up their cross, and identify themselves with His new community.

The results of evangelism include obedience to Christ, incorporation into His church and responsible service in the world.

We hope to persuade men and women, by every means possible, that Jesus is to be treasured above all the world can offer. By the work of evangelism through us, God takes people lower than they have ever been to a sincere and profound realization that they sit at the foot of the cross, heads bowed, awaiting the mercy of God. Then, God elevates these people to the highest office afforded human beings, to being children of God. What a privilege for us to be part of this! What good news for all!

Evangelism and proselytism are two different things. Too many people are slow to enter the ministry of evangelism because it has been reduced to a technique of phrases and pressures that show little respect for the non-Christian. Orlando Costas explains:

> To proselytize is to try to get people to change from one religious belief system, ideology, or political party to another, usually through the offer of psychological, social, cultural, political or economic incentives and through the application of pressure. In contrast, to evangelize is to share with others lovingly and respectfully the joyful news and liberating grace of the gospel, to extend its invitation to faith in Christ and participation in His fellowship, and commit the person or community's response to the Holy Spirit. Authentic evangelization refuses to be coercive and is always respectful of human dignity and freedom because it is an act of love. It is, therefore, against proselytism.[1]

Evangelism is not fast talk aimed at gaining "converts"; it is a ministry of word and deed that leads people to the place where they can activate *their* faith in the person of Jesus. Asking people to enter a relationship with God is a serious thing, and we should not ask them to take it any less seriously than committing to another person for life in marriage.

Ultimately, we do not *do* evangelism. In the final sense, it is God who enters into the life of a human being and by the Holy Spirit draws that person into a love relationship with himself. God has chosen to use us as instruments in this process.

## The Consequences of Evangelism

Evangelicals typically say that the two great consequences of evangelism are the "forgiveness of sins" and "life everlasting." These are certainly two great consequences. The work of evangelism is not only private, however, and we limit its power if we expect it to only change internal lives. Emilio Castro, general secretary of the World Council of Churches, has outlined the radical consequences of evangelism:

> Because the Kingdom is God's mission, fully manifested in the total self-emptying of Jesus Christ, those who listen to the message of the Kingdom are invited to respond in radical discipleship. Conversion is not an option for the pastoral work of the church. It is the only possible answer to the dramatic disclosure of God's passionate love. To proclaim the Kingdom is always an invitation to join the forces of the Kingdom and to enter into the Kingdom. Repentance is the first act of response. Sins are confessed, allegiances changed and attitudes transformed. If the Kingdom is God's plan in action, and if what the Christians experience is the anticipation of that Kingdom that is coming into the actual life of today, then we move in a world of wonder and excitement, a world of final decisions. No other word than conversion would serve here.[2]

Conversion. You and I have been rescued from the kingdom of darkness into the kingdom of light. We have accepted the identity and responsibilities that go with being the people of Jesus. We are no longer private persons, but members of Jesus' army. We have become members of that community of the King that has declared war on every form of evil and abuse that Satan unleashes on individuals and society. Therefore, our entire lives, particularly our relationships with others and the world, must be affected.

Theories such as the homogeneous principle of church growth have not called people to conversion into the kingdom. Encountering Christ in secret while outwardly promoting patterns of racism or economic abuse is not truly encountering Christ. No, conversion must affect every aspect of our lives, public as well as private, and when we lead others to Christ we are leading them to live their dedication to him in public.

In fact, we do not have the right to invite people to Jesus unless it is the historical Jesus. This means we must invite people to serve the Jesus who has always served the "least of these," who has always promoted compassion, justice, and integrity above the pursuit of wealth, comfort, power, and reputation. Jesus told the disciples to go into the world as the Father had sent him (John 20:21). Likewise, we must call people to follow the example of Jesus and do so ourselves.

Because evangelism occurs in concrete circumstances, it affects the world and individuals in terms that are both personally meaningful and publicly obvious. To quote Orlando Costas: "Evangelization involves . . . social and historically situated human beings. . . . There is no such thing as a contemporary man or woman. These are men and women in concrete contemporary situations."[3] The Spirit's transformation of the personal lives and social existence of women and men finds its correspondence in their outward behavior in society and the transformation of their reality.[4]

The evidence that I have met Christ (the consequence of evangelism) is that I have changed. We become evangelists because we believe God calls the church to live as salt, light, and healing in a wicked, dark, and broken world. When we pray for conversion of others, we are praying for no less than a radical dismantling of the systems that crush God's precious and beautiful creations; we are praying for nothing less than peace between warring ethnic groups; we are praying for nothing less than a Zaccheus-like conversion that gives back fourfold what we stole from the poor. We are praying for nothing less than marriages to be healed and for children to be reconciled to parents. We are praying for the welfare of the city.

Evangelism is the most radical notion available to the human experience. We must not reduce it to a simple verbal formula that puts me at peace with ungodly materialism in my life-style because I have mentally accepted eternal bliss. That is not conversion to Jesus but, as my friend Tom Sine says, "the American dream with a Jesus overlay."

True evangelism, then, takes place inside the community of faith. Just as our Christianity is best lived out among a body of believers, evangelism is most effective when it calls people into a relationship with a holy God and into a fellowship of believers. It is here that our life describes the kingdom agenda; it is here that we challenge the kingdom of darkness (in a specific concrete circumstance); and it is here that we provide each other with the necessary fellowship, gifts, and correctives that will help us be effective in the ministry of evangelism.

Christian community development cannot happen without the work of evangelism. The goal of Christian service to the urban poor is not programs that change the environment a little bit here and a little bit there. Instead, we are praying for the Holy Spirit to overturn the powers of darkness. Conversion brings about not only spiritual change but also development in individuals, and as those individuals take leadership, they bring about the development and conversion of others.

The consequence of evangelism is strength and comfort for people crushed by the oppressive conditions of life. Without the love of Jesus in their hearts these people would literally die. The Holy Spirit heals the gashes in our hearts, comforts us in the loss of children ravaged by poverty, and affirms our dignity in the face of dehumanization. Evangelism brings us to Jesus Christ, who understands every way in which the poor suffer abuse, and who comforts us through the Holy Spirit.

Who would deny the urban poor this treasure?

# 8

# WHOLESOME CARE

When Vera Mae and I moved to Southern California in 1982, intending to retire, we heard about a neighborhood in Pasadena that had the highest daytime crime rate in Southern California. A good friend of mine took me to Northwest Pasadena to look at the community. When I returned home, I said, "Vera Mae, I know what we need to do now." We moved to the corner of Howard and Navarro, a place of death, violence, and drugs. When we arrived, we were next door to one of the biggest drug operations around. During peak hours, twenty to thirty cars an hour were arriving to buy drugs. There were tents for prostitution set up in the backyard. Children were getting killed as they ran drugs.

Our hearts were broken that children should have to grow up in an environment like this. We started a prayer meeting in our house and a Good News Club in our garage. Our goal was to rescue the children from the environment around them; but it was also to ultimately change the environment they were in. Today, we own the houses that were once the drug houses. A community church meets in one of them on Sunday. We offer tutoring, recreation, and Bible lessons for the children after school during the week. Over the summer we expand this care in our day camp to six hours a day.

These programs are helping a lot of individual kids, but most important, the community environment is slowly changing. The drug traffic is not nearly so big and public, and the drug houses have closed down. People are starting to take pride in their community. It is getting to be a neighborly place. And now I can see a couple of kids, the kids who live across the street from the Harambee Center, venture out of their fenced-in yards to roller-skate and jump rope and play on the sidewalks.

Once, a *Los Angeles Times* reporter came out to Harambee to spend the day with me. He wanted to write a story about Harambee. At the end of the day, we sat down, he got out his pad and pen, and he asked me, "John, what are you doing here?" I told him, "We are trying to meet the greatest need in this community, which is the need for care. We are trying to parent these children." Then he asked me, "What do you want to achieve?" "I want the kids to be able to play in the street again," I said.

The wholesome care that we are bringing to Northwest Pasadena is central to Christian community development. As I discussed in the previous chapter, our gospel is stunted if we are only concerned about either the physical or the spiritual alone. Indeed, as David Claerbaut has written, "Humans were created to be whole persons, with physical, mental and spiritual dimensions. Deprivation in any of these dimensions has a deadening effect on the others, since all parts are interrelated and interactive. . . . The soul without a body is a ghost; the body without a soul is a corpse."[1]

## Applying Wholesome Care

Of course, no human environment is perfect. Even the Garden of Eden had limits for Adam and Eve (the tree) and evil (the serpent). Some people who think about and do Christian community development have made a perfect community their goal, which is a utopian dream. Other Christians take the opposite attitude, the "lifeboat" mentality: The world is on its way to hell and there is nothing to be done to make it better; we simply have to snatch as many people out of it as we can by preaching.

I believe instead that we must find a balance between working out, by faith, the prayer of our Lord—"Thy kingdom come, Thy will be done in earth, as it is in heaven"(Matt. 6:10 KJV)—and accepting that until the final day of our Lord, evil will be present throughout society. As Christians, we should not go to either extreme. Christian community development is centered around people. We know that constructing a perfect society is impossible, but we cannot ignore God's commands to be salt and light to the world and to care for orphans and widows. That is exactly what we pray that our presence in Northwest Pasadena will do—be a light of hope amid the darkness of hopelessness and despair.

We have learned over thirty-five years of living and working among the poor that it is difficult to be salt and light if we ignore the concrete realities of people's environment. The gospel addresses us in our specific situations and reaches out to us in our places of need. While people are not simply products of their environment, environment most definitely has a significant impact in shaping each one of us.

## Creating an Environment of Hope

Every place of need is unique. There is no "master plan of community development"; community development must be worked out in a local situation. At Harambee, we identified the most important needs and designed our plan to meet them. I do want to list, however, some aspects of the environment of the urban poor that Christian community development should try to address. An expert social worker tries to understand all of the factors that produce a healthy environment for personal development. I want to highlight eight of these factors, not in any particular order. Other practical suggestions for ways to meet these needs will be given in chapter nine.

### *Dignity*

It is hard to describe, really, but when you have spent your whole lifetime with limited opportunities, being told your place is at the bottom, you end up with a low image of yourself.

We do not confer dignity upon other human beings. God has already given dignity to us when he created us. We are his personal handiwork; what greater source of dignity could we have? We can, however, suppress or crush in others their understanding of their dignity. Historical dehumanization of a group of people combined with an individual's current experience of being dehumanized effectively suppresses that person's sense of personal dignity.

Historically we blacks were treated by whites like animals valued for labor. I as a black man could not have legally been a father until the late 1800s, only 125 years ago. Similarly, women could not legally be mothers, but instead were maids and nannies as well as baby machines and sexual objects for white men. Middle-class white America's heritage is folklore of the noble struggle for independence from England, heroic exploration of the West, and rags-to-riches stories of building a Fortune 500 company from a corner newspaper stand by hard work and good management. We blacks, however, share a history of slavery, sharecropping, forced segregation, suppression of human status (two-thirds human, legally speaking), and humiliation. What made this even worse was that often the white masters and overseers who were treating us blacks like subhumans were also our ministers and Sunday school teachers.

At Harambee, we see some of the negative effects of this history. Many of our children, both black and Mexican-American, struggle with negative self-image. For some, this moves them to fight or to rebel in other ways. We make it a point to affirm the dignity of the people around us, particularly the children. We teach ethnic history lessons in the after-school program, so that children can be proud of their heritage. When we need to discipline the children, we are careful to do so in ways that build them up and encourage them. Our Harambee creed, which the children learn in the after-school program, sums up the attitude we take and try to give to the children:

We are what we make of ourselves.
We will no longer fit into the mold that has been prepared for us.
We will strive for a completeness in Christ that compels us to stand against the social and economic injustices of our time.
We will identify and understand our heritage, thus affirming our family.
We will learn to use the economic system to free our people from the poverty cycle.
We will never discourage, but always encourage, our brothers and sisters.
Then, we will join hands and move together to change our society.
HARAMBEE! HARAMBEE! Let's get together and push!

## Power

Many middle- and upper-class people expect that honest, hard work will result in wealth. This promise is what fuels the American dream. The urban poor do not have this same expectation. The historical legacy of hard work benefiting only the slave master, the boss man, or the wealthy landowner still takes away initiative that in today's America could produce a better-quality life. To the poor, it seems that their situation is the same regardless of what they do.

City governments are unresponsive to the needs of the urban poor. City works departments that exist to attend to roads, electricity, water, power, waste disposal, and building standards are quicker and more likely to serve the middle-class taxpayer.

After Vera Mae and I had just acquired the main drug house on Navarro, it was going to be inspected. The drug dealers who had lived there had trashed it, and their water had been shut off because they hadn't paid the bill. We wanted to get the house cleaned up before the inspectors came, so I turned the water on in order to clean up and then turned it back off.

When I went down to city hall to get the water officially turned on, the black girl who greeted me at the desk told me that there was a $400 fine for turning on the water unofficially. I hadn't known that such a law existed, and I thought it was ridiculous. "I'm not a poor person, and I won't pay that," I said to her. She went back to get her supervisor. When she brought her supervisor out, I'm sure she was surprised. Her supervisor, a white woman, said, "Oh, hello, Reverend Perkins. I enjoyed your sermon very much last Sunday. What can I do for you?" I explained that I wanted the water turned on, and the supervisor said, "We'll do that right away." The girl who had greeted me asked, "What about the fine?" Her supervisor said, "Oh, don't worry about it."

Because I was known, and because my visible commitment to my community has made me into a person with "power," I was spared having to pay a ridiculous fine that the typical urban poor citizen would not have the influence to avoid.

The urban poor also experience powerlessness in the face of the law. Because of the disproportionate amount of crime in poor urban areas, many times law enforcement officers, whose job it is to serve and protect, lump all the urban poor into the category of criminal. While wealthy residents understand how to use the system, in too many cases the poor do not. Their typical view of the law is negative. In most of their dealings with legal structures they more likely experience the cold, exacting judgment of the legal system in critical times of need. Evictions, denial of various permits, and cold social workers are the ways the poor usually encounter the law and the legal structures. This system frequently reinforces a poverty mentality and increases their sense of powerlessness.

### Education

The United Nations and other global nongovernmental agencies describe many parts of the Third World as currently in an educational crisis. They describe America's urban poor in the same language. The crisis in education has two aspects in America's ghettos: The quality of public education is falling, and the urban poor no longer value education.

Poor education has many obvious consequences: underemployment or unemployment, poor nutrition, bad housing conditions, ill health, bad retirement, and powerlessness to use the system for one's benefit. Many seventeen-year-old children in the ghettos cannot read or write. As a result, they cannot understand their legal obligations and privileges; they cannot interpret a lease agreement, a vehicle purchase agreement, a driver's test, a health directive, or an announcement of community services that would help them develop such skills. Many of our neighborhood children who come to Harambee for tutoring cannot read first-grade books, although they are in fifth or sixth grade. Their tutors discover this because the children are not following directions on their homework. When the tutors ask why, they learn that the children cannot read the directions.

In America, education and quality of life are directly related. Lacking a good education means lacking, among other things, access to the very doorway that leads to a wholesome life-style. Education is not a luxury in modern American society—it is essential for survival.

Many of our children are getting a poor education because of the problems of our inner-city public schools. Most suburban public schools prepare their students for college or vocational school. An

94

*Our Gospel*

honest survey of inner-city schools, however, should raise questions about the city's commitment to the poor as well as sound the alarm on the problems our nation will face tomorrow for neglecting this urgent responsibility today.

Classroom discipline is an increasing problem, with teachers being expected to handle classes of thirty or more students, many of whom come from dysfunctional homes and bring their anger and troubles to an often insensitive and unsympathetic environment. The low status and pay of teachers as well as the lack of support and appreciation drive many people out of teaching and discourage our most gifted young adults from entering it in the first place. This problem is especially great in inner-city schools. As a result, the challenges of teaching, which demand all the talent we can muster for it, are not being met. Children are promoted from grade to grade without ever learning the basic skills they need to function effectively, preventing them from taking advantage of the upper grades. Simply holding them back does not address the reasons they did not learn those skills to begin with.

Some school programs seem to be designed with no concern for the education of the students. One child who comes to Harambee for tutoring brought her math homework for her tutor to check. It was obvious to the tutor that this little girl did not understand how to add fractions; she had simply added the numerators together and added the denominators, so that $\frac{1}{4} + \frac{2}{3} = \frac{3}{7}$. The tutor, in trying to explain how to add fractions, discovered that the girl did not understand what a fraction was, did not understand that one-fourth of four eggs was one egg. The tutor asked this little girl what she had been studying about math in school. "Well, I'm only in math two days a week, because I go to a special language arts program all day three days a week," the girl answered. "Do you mean you miss math three days a week? Are you doing the same thing as the rest of the class?" the tutor asked. This girl was being expected to keep up with her class in math while being prevented from hearing even half of the class sessions.

Another girl was absent from school one Monday. The next day, she came to Harambee explaining that she didn't have any homework for the week. "My teacher told me that since I had missed Monday, I wouldn't be able to do the homework for the week," the girl said. Her tutor asked her how her teacher expected her to be able to keep up with the class. "Oh, we're just going to do the same thing again next week," was her reply. These incidents are not isolated or unusual. We need to take a good hard look at how our schools are teaching our children and keep the schools accountable.

Parents and communities are just as responsible as the schools for the decline in education. Many, if not most, of the urban poor have ceased to value education because they do not see that it pays off. When parents are not educated, they frequently do not expect their children to work hard in school, and they do not make sure that their children do their homework. In fact, antagonism can build up between the teacher and the parent, with the result that the parent will not back up the teacher if the child is causing disciplinary problems.

The extreme example of this in my own community involves two brothers whom I'll call Steve and Joe. Steve is twelve, going on thirteen; Joe is a couple of years younger. Most of their male relatives are drug dealers; their mother is an alcoholic. Both of them steal and fight and are negative leaders for the rest of the kids on the block.

Steve is almost entirely illiterate. He has basically not gone to school for the last three years. Last fall, he came to Derek and said that he wanted to change. He wanted to stop going down the road to jail and death. He wanted to be a Christian. He was sincere, too. So, we enrolled him in a local Christian school where he would get a lot of individual attention. We went to his house every morning to pick him up to go to school. One morning when we got to the house, he wouldn't come out, and his mother refused to make him go to school. She said, "He's old enough to decide for himself if he wants to go to school."

Imagine! At twelve, an illiterate boy is old enough in his mother's eyes to decide for himself that he's not going to go to school. After a month, we stopped trying to get him to school. His brother Joe has not been in school all year either. Until recently, we never heard Joe communicate except in grunts. We never heard him put a whole sentence together. We think he has started communicating more because we have been showing love to him, because now he feels that he has some significance.

Some of the other children who come to our tutoring program to do their homework go home to mothers who are sitting around drinking with men who are playing dice and smoking dope. The TV, radio, or both are blaring until late at night. No child could get to sleep early enough in this environment to go to school well-rested, much less with homework finished. Their mothers seem to be completely unaware of what kind of environment an elementary school child needs in order to thrive.

Most critically, educators all over the country are telling us that the most crucial years in a child's educational development occur long before the child ever gets to public school—those crucial years are the first years of life. Most of our urban parents are not spending time reading to their children and giving them healthy stimulation that helps their brains develop; instead, they are putting their children in front of the TV or simply neglecting them.

In addition, we have an epidemic of babies born addicted to the various drugs that their mothers are using. My son Derek can point to several children who attend our program whom he calls "crack babies." Such children are often disruptive and can only concentrate for short periods of time. Some are even mildly to severely retarded.

We have failed to take advantage of the educational system at the community level. When families fail to take responsibility for their children's education, the community has to step in to take that responsibility. Neighbors need to call truant officers about children who aren't in school. Community adults need to encourage children to excel educationally, to provide role models of educated people, and to reinforce the school system when possible (or provide an alternative if needed). Concerned Christians need to befriend the parents of dysfunctional families in order to win their trust. Only after winning their trust can you step in and help with the education of their children. Here at Harambee, we are trying to win the trust of the parents, tutor neighborhood children, and communicate to both over and over again the importance of education.

### *Employment*

It comes as no surprise that the nation's poorest are also the nation's unemployed. Someone who is poor for the first time probably arrived at that status through unemployment. The chronically poor, however, are unemployed because they are unprepared. Lack of education, skill development, and opportunity are all qualities of poverty and are direct factors leading to unemployment. One who lives with these circumstances enters a cycle of poverty where poverty leads to unpreparedness, which leads to unemployment, which leads to poverty, and so forth. The cycle has to be interrupted, but that is not easily achieved. The "culture" of the unemployed urban black male, especially, teaches that work does not come easily and when it does, does not reward financially. The minimum wage, for example, does not provide enough to cover rent, utilities, groceries, and transport; thus, taking one of these jobs is not an attractive option.

The other side of the employment dilemma is that a lot of young black men choose either to earn quick money through selling drugs or to live off their girlfriends' welfare checks (or paychecks), and ghetto culture has accepted that. The lure of making risky but quick drug money is doing as much harm to the overall development of our black men as the drugs themselves. This attraction, with its short-term mentality, is one of the things that is taking away from the ghettos the will to work. Our boys grow up today without many (if any) employed male role models. The national black role models they have are almost all entertainers or sports stars. Some even secretly admire the instant success of the drug pushers.

Most of the young boys who come to Harambee say they are going to be football or basketball players when they grow up. Boys focused on a sports career, unless they have a parent or parents who demand that they keep other options open, often neglect school and focus on athletics. They then discover when they get to high school that they aren't good enough to make the college team, or if they make a college team, they discover after four years of little education and a lot of sports that they are not good enough to make the pros.

To be sure, there are many people in the ghettos who are working; but there are not enough, and there are not enough enterprises in the ghettos. Indigenous enterprises are crucial to employment. They provide role models who are working, and role models demonstrate what is involved in having a job, show that young people should work, and provide valuable contact with the working world. Enterprises provide job opportunities, which are also opportunities to develop skills and to get work experience. Work experience is almost required now to get a job, which makes it very difficult to get a first job.

In our neighborhood, few of the adults work. When I work in my yard during the afternoon, there are always a few kids who want to help me. Some want to help me for money, but others want to help me just to be helping. They don't have a role model at home with whom they can work, who can teach them to work, and I think they sense they need this. If we can instill in our people the value and will to work and if we can give our people good employment options and help them become employable, we can and most likely will help them free themselves from poverty.

### *Health*

After salary, the most commonly asked question in America at job interviews is, "What are the health benefits?" Middle-class America understands the need for good health, and it understands that health care is so costly that it will be unaffordable unless provided by the employer.

The link between poverty and health is simple. First, the poor rarely have the knowledge or resources common to middle-class America for preventive care, such as a healthy diet and simple life-style measures that can lead to a healthier body. Compare the diet of the urban poor to that of middle America, and you will see that ghetto residents eat much more "junk" food and generally have a much poorer diet nutritionally, although most of them have enough to eat.

Cities are also unhealthy places to live. Often, the cheapest housing is located in smog-producing industrial locations. In addition, crowded living conditions (the poor often live three families to a home) result in constant exposure to other people's sickness. Poverty often means no heat during the cold winter months. Sewers clog up and are left unattended by disinterested landlords or municipal governments.

When emergencies occur, the poor cannot afford to pay for essential services, and over a lifetime, debilitating conditions can result. While a well-employed middle-class citizen produces an insurance card at a suburban hospital and receives care, the inner-city emergency room closes down due to lack of funds and the poor are often refused any but the bare minimum of treatment without insurance. Only some form of a national health plan will give our urban poor adequate medical attention and help break the cycle of poverty perpetuated by ill health. Few legislators, driven by money and power, have grasped the seriousness of the situation; therefore, the poor are without a voice. It is the church who is to be the mouthpiece of the poor.

Steve Crane, a young white doctor serving at Voice of Calvary's Health Center in Jackson, Mississippi, has devoted his life to serving the health care needs of the poor in our nation's poorest state. In addition to giving quality personal care to individual patients, Steve has also lobbied on behalf of his patients and others like them. In 1989 a local church denomination-operated hospital in which many poor mothers received prenatal care and gave birth to their babies announced the closing of its obstetrics wing and its relocation to a suburban hospital. To the owners of the hospital it was strictly a business decision. Because of its many Medicaid patients, the obstetrics wing of the hospital did not make enough profit. Some wealthy patients even complained about sharing facilities with poor people.

But for the poor, with whom Steve worked, the closing would have disastrous consequences. How would these mothers on Medicaid receive the care they need, and where would they deliver their babies? These were not profit and loss questions to Steve and the Voice of Calvary Health Center; the women and babies who would suffer had names and faces. In lobbying against this injustice, Voice of Calvary stood to lose some of its local support. But for people concerned about equal access to health care for the poor, there was no other choice but to step out front and take the heat that followed. To the praise of God, the hospital eventually decided to keep the obstetrics wing. Steve says we will never know if speaking out and calling attention to this situation made any difference in the decision. The bottom line was that the poor continued to receive the care they desperately needed.

### *Security*

When exposés of police brutality erupt on the front pages of our papers, they demonstrate why the urban poor do not have a good feeling about the police motto "to serve and protect." In the minds of many urban blacks, "to serve and protect" applies only to the white upper and middle classes. Most blacks find themselves the constant object of police suspicion.

Black urban poor do not feel secure around most police. Rather, we fear them (and for solid reasons). We in Pasadena are somewhat of an exception to this. We have a good relationship with our police chief because he is a good man. Because he grew up in projects where the police were viewed as the enemy, he determined to show another way when he got the chance to lead. I am very grateful for this good relationship. I can call on our police chief when I need to, but I know this is not common. In addition, inner-city police forces are usually understaffed and underequipped compared with suburban forces—they simply are not able to respond to the needs of those inner-city people who face burglary, muggings, and rape.

Psychiatrists have studied children who grow up in "violence cultures" (such as Lebanon) and confirm the long-term negative impact of such an environment. The poor of urban America are reared under similar circumstances. Prolonged exposure to violence and the fear of its consequences permanently damage the emotions and psyche of young, innocent children. These children have been robbed of the security that should accompany youth, and because of it are emotionally insecure.

Forming neighborhood watches and organizing communities against drug sales and other such activities are ways to combat the immediate problems. The best long-term solution is to develop the youth, enabling them to have alternatives to these destructive life-styles.

### *Recreation*

We require rest. We need times of rejuvenation and recreation of our spirits. God established the Sabbath not only for worship of him but also for rest. And yet the ghetto environment is not restful. It is rarely quiet or peaceful. The atmosphere is tense, waiting for a conflict of some kind to break out. Safety is always an issue for children playing or adults relaxing outside. Most inner cities are crowded with tall buildings, leaving little or no open space for children to play in or for adults to relax in. In the Tenderloin district in inner-city San

Francisco, there is just one tiny park with no grassy space and a side-walk cutting diagonally through it; there are only a few benches for people to sit on.

It is often hard for the people of the inner city to get out of the neighborhood for recreation. Most inner-city children never go more than a couple of miles from where they live. They have seen other environments on TV, but they have not been able to experience them. At Harambee, we take kids camping, horseback riding, to the park—anywhere in nature—on the weekends. Adults need this change of scene, too, but something especially significant happens to kids when they are able to get into the outdoors, away from TV and the culture of the city streets, away from destructive home situations. They are able to take the joy that all children should have in just playing, enjoying themselves as children should, without being pushed prematurely into an adult view of the world.

For our unemployed young men, it may seem that their entire lives are recreation, but their activities do not bring the kind of refreshment that wholesome recreation after satisfying work brings. In addition to employment, they need activities like sports that can be a positive outlet for their energy. In the same way, our teenagers, while they are in school, need recreational activities that will keep them occupied and interested in their free time; otherwise, their recreational time will hang heavy on their hands and draw them into crime.

Suburban kids are usually kept busy from a young age with music lessons, Boy and Girl Scouts, family weekend activities, organized sports, and all kinds of challenging, fun, useful ways to spend time. At Harambee we try to keep our children busy with fun and useful activities from after school until dinnertime, as well as many weekends. We also provide a basketball hoop (there is a game going on every day after school) and open space to play in. That is as important as anything else we do.

### Beauty

Quality Christian community development is not just interested in people's survival. We want our lives to reflect all that is good and all that reflects the handiwork of our God. The same Creator who made us made his creation beautiful. We pursue beauty because God has created us in his image and because our spirits are refreshed and energized as we encounter God in beauty. Living in an ugly environment is depressing and makes us less likely to care about that environment. Some urban children are growing up without an appreciation for beauty because they see so few examples of it.

Beauty is increasingly becoming something that only the wealthy have easy access to. Museums, botanical gardens, beautiful buildings, and parks are almost never found in the inner city and frequently cost money to enter, while inner-city neighborhoods are becoming more and more run-down.

It is a priority to us at Harambee to keep our facility attractive and neat, so that it is a cheerful and refreshing place to come. We strive to encourage the appreciation of beauty in our young people. Because I love flowers, I have planted a lot of flowers in the yard. Our neighborhood kids see me taking care of them, and because they care for me, they see that the flowers are important and admire them. They pick our flowers. I let them pick the flowers because I feel that they should be able to enjoy that beauty. Children who are able to interact with beauty, to enjoy beauty, have something very precious.

When Vera Mae was sick, our Harambee kids would come and visit her. They would come to sing for her and to bring the flowers they had picked from our yard. Her room was already filled with flowers that people had sent her, but the flowers the kids brought were extra special. Some of the older kids also made hearts out of paper and strung them on a string that she hung in her room. She still keeps those hearts in our room today.

When God called Abraham to bless him, and to bless all the nations through him, he employed the notion of "Shalom." This Hebrew word, in time, came to mean everything good you would want for yourself and wishing that same quality of life for your neighbors and friends. We have been called to be a blessing to the urban poor, a blessing that includes everything that is good and wholesome. Our notions of Christian community development will look different from place to place, but some of the essential blessings we are called to bestow on the poor include dignity, power, education, employment, health, security, recreation, and beauty. The world will run to a church that loves in such a wholesome manner as this.

# 9

# PROVIDING SERVICES

Central to the failure of the welfare system is the fact that it tried to fit a fixed "solution" on all the nation's poor, doing very little to answer specific concrete needs at the local level. While work among the urban poor is often thought of in terms of providing social programs and services for the poor, the effect of social programs on a community is mixed. Programs or services benefit a local community only to the degree that they come from the "bottom up," that is, reflect the actual felt needs of the people being served. Because the needs and the people of every community are different, programs designed for Chicago are unlikely to fit Miami.

If programs and services are done for a community, rather than with and by the people of the community, these programs do not help the people of the community develop. They simply continue the mentality of dependency that the welfare state has created in so many of our urban centers and that suppresses the dignity of the people there. In Christian community development, we want to empower people to take responsibility for their own lives and to have the consciousness of their own dignity and worth that comes from being able to have such control. In order to do so, we need to give responsibility for programs at least in part to them.

In this chapter, to illustrate the ideas in this book, I will describe some programs that have worked in some places. I hope these suggestions will give you ideas for involving the people of your community in enriching their own neighborhoods. I have organized them by the eight characteristics outlined in chapter eight. You and your church will probably come up with other ideas as your local community of faith dreams with the help of the Holy Spirit.

## Dignity

Ethnic heritage and history have traditionally not been valued by mainstream American society. Although this is starting to change, many ethnic people still feel a lack of pride in their own heritage that contributes to a low self-image. Affirming the heritage of your community is thus an important part of affirming its dignity.

If your work takes you into an ethnic group other than your own, study their history, heroes, achievements, contributions to society, and role models for advancement and success. Demonstrating that you think their heritage is important will give your neighbors additional pride in it. In your own ethnic group, it is that much easier to demonstrate the value of ethnic heritage. Encourage ethnic pride among the children. Organize celebrations of important ethnic holidays or historical events.

February is national Black Heritage Month. If you live in a black neighborhood, this is the time to sponsor a block-wide party, complete with band and barbecue, celebrating the contributions of blacks to American life. Prominent local black businesspeople and community activists can be invited to give inspiring speeches concerning black history, well-known black athletes from nearby universities can come to give autographs, and black professors from universities could be present to model the value of education. Invite local black-operated businesses to put up stands to sell their goods and encourage the sale of items that reinforce black heritage: posters of famous black men and women, black arts and crafts, black-authored books, and black music (CDs and tapes). Ask the mayor or chief of police to give a word of welcome and have the local fire station park a fire engine, staffed by their black staff, near the event.

It is very easy to underestimate the value to children of seeing positive role models. It has been our experience that black kids seeing black faces in traditional jobs (such as firefighters) have proven to be very inspirational. The same principles apply to other ethnic groups.

In a Latino neighborhood, celebrate Cinco de Mayo (the Fifth of May). In a multi-ethnic neighborhood, such as ours, celebrate both.

In addition to ethnic pride, encourage your neighbors to take pride in the local community. At Harambee, we sponsor a block party once a year in order to encourage a sense of neighborhood cohesiveness. Our neighbors have come to expect it, and every year, folks ask me, "Are we having the block party again this year? When?" Our block parties are great fun. We get a permit from city hall to block off the street all day Saturday, we get local bands to come, we provide games, and we get our junior high and high school kids to sell food at reduced prices. It is a great time to bring everyone together and to continue building relationships with our neighbors.

Giving positive affirmation to people in a vacuum can and does sometimes become patronizing. Mushy positive reinforcement without discipline can do as much harm as good. We have witnessed many whites who have come to help the "poor black kids" and have allowed the children to manipulate their guilt so that they can go undisciplined. In many cases the children will prefer and gravitate to the people who will hold them less accountable. So please be careful with your affirmation to make sure that it is a healthy mix of unconditional love and discipline.

## Power

The methods of community activism developed in the 1960s and 1970s, which I participated in, accomplished many good things. Often, an unjust government must be openly confronted for change to take place. This confrontational method has its downside, however. It produces antagonism between local government and the people. This should be avoided when it can be. I have found in Pasadena, and many other CCDA members have found in their various communities, that it is not only possible but also desirable to work together with officials, to make friends with them and gain their support for our work of community development. In Pasadena, we have been able to elect many city officials, a city director, and several school board members who knew that their election depended on Northwest Pasadena. By treating them as friends rather than as enemies, we are able to keep them more accountable to their promises.

We know that they will listen to us when we need them to. In Peoria, Illinois, Stan Maclin, the leader of a CCDA ministry, actually served on the city council for a number of years.

I am not saying that we should accept injustice within the governing system or that we should, because officials are our friends, look the other way when they are wrong. What I am saying is that if we are friends with our city officials, we can keep them accountable to doing justice as a friend can keep a friend accountable. We can give them constructive criticism about public services and tell them how those services can better serve us, without having the conversation turn into a confrontation. They will be more likely to listen to us if they know that we want to work with them rather than against them.

In addition, working with officials takes away the attitude that government should do everything for us. I believe that government should make it possible for us to do things for ourselves. By having a good working relationship with city officials, we can say to them, "We of Northwest Pasadena would like to see this happen, and we are willing to do this work in order to make it happen. How can you help us and what suggestions do you have for us?" If we take responsibility to carry out our dreams, we have a greater sense of ownership and more pride in the results.

Of course, there will be some city officials in some places who will refuse to act justly, who may be outright racists, or who care nothing for the poor. We need to work to remove these people from office. I believe, however, that in most situations, the political climate of the 1990s is such that we can have a greater influence on the rest of the government to remove these people if we have a good working relationship with the government as a whole. We should always strive to speak the truth in love.

Bearing this in mind, let me give some suggestions for ways of empowering our urban communities. One of the most important things we did at Harambee soon after we arrived in the neighborhood was to sponsor a series of "listening meetings." These meetings were an opportunity for neighborhood residents to meet together with city officials, school board members, and others to discuss the problems they saw. Such meetings can easily turn into gripe sessions that accomplish very little other than to antagonize people.

I was very careful, as the moderator, to keep the meetings focused not on voicing complaints but on thinking of solutions that would give responsibility to the people of the neighborhood as well as the government. The meetings kept the city government aware of the needs of Northwest Pasadena and particularly how it could help us carry out our own ideas.

Another important part of empowering neighborhood people is getting them involved in existing government decision-making processes. Government officials do not always have to come to us; we can go to them. Most civil service organizations have regular public meetings that few people from the inner city attend because they don't know about them and don't know what role they would play at these meetings. Find out about and publicize the agendas and times of city council meetings, school board meetings, Parent-Teacher Association meetings, police commission meetings, and so on. Encourage your neighbors to go to these meetings. Invite them to go along with you.

Ask an elected official from your district to come to the community and explain how citizens can give input. (The official will probably be glad to gain visibility in the community.) Maybe someone from the church can drive a church van to the school board meeting while one or two of the neighbors take care of everyone's kids. And don't underestimate the intelligence of your neighbors. Chances are they will recognize legislation or policies that will have a negative impact on them. Encourage them to voice these concerns directly to officials and organize the neighborhood to write letters or make phone calls protesting these policies. At election time, invite the candidates into your neighborhood for community meetings, encourage your neighbors to voice their concerns, be visible about voting, and then work to keep elected officials accountable to their campaign promises.

When involving the community in local government, the more leadership that is taken by your neighbors rather than you, the better. Don't let your church or ministry staff become the substitute for local people taking responsibility and leadership themselves. Meetings that are small enough should be held in homes rather than at the church or ministry building; this increases the sense of ownership. And when organizing people, strive for unity around a specific need. Bring the people who feel a certain need together, and don't try to bring everyone else in out of a desire to have the whole community present.

If you are careful to make the issues known in a way that makes people feel that it is possible for them to have some impact, the people who care about those issues and are willing to take responsibility for them will come forward. You may initially have to spend a lot of time encouraging your community members individually that they are capable of having an impact; that's what the "listening meetings" at Harambee accomplished. Once people have discovered that they can take control of their own lives, do not stand in their way.

Another way to help your neighbors gain greater control of their lives is to connect them with church members who can serve as advocates and mediators. Tenant-landlord conflicts are common in the inner city. Perhaps a Christian lawyer or experienced mediator in your community or from an outside church that supports your ministry can come together with landlord and tenants in listening meetings like the ones I mentioned earlier. These meetings should clarify the rent agreements and responsibilities of tenants and landlord, if necessary, and then discuss solutions to any problems.

I want to stress again that these meetings need to be moderated in a way that keeps them focused on finding solutions and taking mutual responsibility rather than simply complaining. If a landlord refuses to consider the needs of tenants and legal recourse is necessary, then it should be taken; but conflict should not be sought for its own sake. In the same way, mediation and advocacy can be helpful between employers and employees. The goal of such mediation should always be to make it possible for the people of the neighborhood to have more control and to take more responsibility for their own situation.

Advocacy is also important when the people of your neighborhood have conflicts with the law. When your neighbors are being treated unfairly by the justice system, mobilize people within the community of faith to come to their aid. When they have broken the law and need to be held responsible, even more advocacy and community support are needed.

Let's be honest. When you are involved with the urban poor, there will be times when some will have to face the consequences of their transgressions. If we are to be trusted as advocates then truth must be at the center of our advocacy. It does no one any good when we excuse the wrongdoings of our kids because we love them. It is sometimes more loving to encourage them to face the consequences of their actions. In my community, the Harambee staff and I have often gone to court with our neighborhood kids when they were arrested for stealing or other crimes. This has made it possible for the judges to release the kids into our custody. In the same way, when young people or adults in your neighborhood have to go to court, rally the neighbors and the community of faith behind them. If the parent of a family has to go to jail, find people in the community to care for their kids, visit them in prison, take care of their apartment or house, and support them in whatever specific ways they need to be supported. If they have to pay a fine they can't afford, the church may be able to loan it to them in return for some kind of service. If they have to do community service, try to find ways for them to do it in their own immediate community.

Finally, do not ignore the power of prayer. We have recently begun a neighborhood prayer meeting in Northwest Pasadena with our Christian neighbors, and it is exciting to see how people respond to the responsibility of praying for their community.

## Education

The statistics are overwhelming as to the sad state of our inner-city schools. Children coming out of these schools are less prepared to compete with their counterparts who have attended suburban or private schools. Outside of providing our inner-city kids an alternative, we need to be doing what we can to ensure that they get the best education possible in less than ideal situations. One way that has proven effective for us is to give the children extra support through after-school tutoring programs.

The individual attention provided through programs like our Harambee after-school program may be all that is needed to boost a failing student. Poll your neighborhood to find out the educational needs, then recruit volunteer tutors from your neighborhood and local churches for a regularly scheduled tutoring program. Volunteers who can teach music and the arts, as well as those who can handle the core subjects, will produce a strong tutoring program. For elementary-school children, often all that is needed is time with an adult for encouragement and checking homework. Self-confidence and self-discipline are what many children need the most, and tutors can model and encourage these qualities. Regular contact with both parents and teachers of the students enables tutors to reinforce the existing education and to be sensitive to the home environment.

An awards banquet every semester that includes parents and school teachers is a great way to recognize hard work and achievement. Local businesses can be approached for tutoring equipment, such as chairs, books, computers, pens, and chalkboards.

One of the things that came out of our listening meetings was that Paul Gibson, a black man who used to be on the InterVarsity staff in our area, set up a tutoring program at one of the Pasadena elementary schools. This program was so successful that the schools have now adopted his strategy and turned it into part of their program.

In addition, encouraging contact between parents and teachers is crucial. Most, if not all, teachers agree that the most important element in a child's success in school is parental involvement. If parents find it hard to get to parent-teacher meetings because they need child care or transportation, help neighborhood parents share rides and watch each other's children. If some parents are apathetic about their children's education, encourage them to be involved, get their neighbors to encourage them, or, if necessary, bring together the adults of the community who are willing to take collective responsibility for all the neighborhood children and brainstorm ways to serve as "parents" to those children in their education.

At Harambee, two of the most important things we do is support those parents who are parenting their children and serve as parents to those children whose parents are not. One of the boys who comes to Harambee is constantly getting into fights at school, and his mother does very little about it. His teacher is very grateful that she can call my son Derek, tell him about this boy's problems and progress, and know that Derek will deal with this little boy like a father. Other parents are very concerned that their children receive good grades, but they are unable to help their children because they have to work or do not have enough education themselves. They appreciate our partnering with them, and they are very supportive of us.

A much costlier and more challenging, though sometimes necessary, approach to education is for the community of faith to establish its own local private school for the children of the neighborhood. Such a school can offer smaller classes and Christian instruction. Since it is directed and staffed by people who understand the needs of the community and since it is based in the community, it can develop young leaders better than a public school can.

My daughter Priscilla, my son Derek, and Julie Ragland are working toward their vision of a neighborhood school for our local children. Priscilla is working on a Ph.D. in school administration and Julie is earning master's degrees in special education and cross-cultural education. They are looking for dedicated Christian teachers who feel called to teach in the community of need. This school will begin with preschool and go up through eighth grade, although it will start with just preschool, kindergarten, and first grade and add a grade or two every year.

We are beginning a fund that will endow each student's place in the school so that the school will not be dependent on tuition to survive. Although we will always ask each student's parents to pay what they can, sometimes we will want to enroll in the school neighborhood children whose parents do not care enough or are unable to pay. We also plan to have a dormitory for some children who come from destructive home environments.

Some people are concerned that private Christian schools have a negative impact on the public schools. This is a very understandable concern. The May 1991 issue of the *Atlantic Monthly* pointed out that only 3 percent of the children attending the twenty-five worst-rated city school systems are white—meaning that white flight and the deterioration of the public schools have coincided with each other. Inner-city Christian schools should not be another way of running away from the problems of the cities as were some private and suburban schools in the past. On the contrary, it should be one way of attacking the problem. Although we cannot take on the responsibility of educating all our inner-city kids, we can do it for some. When and if this causes Christians to turn their backs on the majority of urban children (such as not supporting school bonds designed to improve city schools), then it becomes a problem. Our desire is for all of the children to get the best quality education.

It has been my experience that bringing in such a school actually improves the quality of education in that area. One reason is as old as America itself—competition. Quality alternatives to the public schools demand that the public schools offer quality education. Second, many of the children we expect to teach are those who would otherwise be dropouts. If our children are falling through the cracks, if their educational needs are not being met, we must do what is needed to educate them. We must do what is necessary to break the self-perpetuating cycle: Because you are poor you get a poor education, because you are less educated you will not be prepared, and because you are less prepared you remain poor.

## Employment

There are two parts to the employment problem. The easiest part to deal with is empowering people to work who want to work. In order to do this, people need to acquire skills that fit the needs of local businesses. It is good to ask the local business community: If we tutored the local community in specific skills, what skills would most closely fit your business needs? Also, look for volunteers in the church, both in the immediate neighborhood and in the wider community, who are willing to take on apprentices at their jobs, provide summer jobs to junior high and high school students, or teach a skill if your city does not have a good skills-training program. If there is a good skills-training program in your city and your neighbors are not using it, find out what is preventing your neighbors from taking advantage of it, and see what solutions can be found.

A program developed out of the Harambee listening meetings was WorkNet. WorkNet is a job development program that recognizes that people need not only a specific marketable skill but also the general skills involved in applying for, getting, and holding down a job. The WorkNet program teaches people what an employer expects of an employee (punctuality, responsibility, reliability, and so on), what an employee can expect of an employer, how to handle a job interview, and what sorts of employment are available. WorkNet provides a telephone number and an address through which businesses can reach WorkNet clients, many of whom do not have a telephone or a permanent address. The WorkNet counselor then stays involved with the client through an initial six-month period on the job, helping the client deal with the new and unfamiliar experiences of the job, serving as a mediator with the employer if necessary, and encouraging the client to stick with the job. Such support is crucial to people who lack proper role models.

Harambee also has a Junior Staff program that employs a number of our local teenagers during the summer. Again, the Junior Staff experience teaches our children, many of whom lack role models, what it means to work and to do a quality job. Their pay is docked if they do a poor job, if they are not punctual, or if they break site rules. They are evaluated during and at the end of the summer. They receive some computer skills training; they take field trips to work sites and colleges; they hear speakers from the Christian business community; and they participate in a Bible teaching time focused on issues of marriage, family, and work. Half of their pay is set aside in a savings account for trade school or college.

Some of the best long-term solutions to the employment problem are businesses based in the community of need. These businesses flow money through rather than out of the community, they raise up working people as role models for the community, and they give their owners the pride and responsibility of working for themselves rather than for someone else.

The other, more difficult side of the problem is how to motivate people to work who do not want to work. I would say that in my community, nearly everyone who wants to work is working. (This is certainly not true of all urban communities.) There is an excellent skills center in Pasadena, but most of the unemployed people of our community do not take advantage of it. Most of the people in our neighborhood who are not working are not interested in WorkNet. Drug dealing is an attractive way to make quick money. As we develop relationships with people, we can encourage them to work by modeling the benefits of employment.

## Health

Both preventive and therapeutic health care programs are needed. One of the more urgent needs today is prenatal care for pregnant women. Some studies suggest that as many as 90 percent of urban poor pregnant women receive no prenatal care. The effects of this, particularly poor nutrition, include injury to the mother, and perhaps even death, and developmental damage to the fetus. While infant death may result, more often brain damage to the fetus occurs.

Dr. Gary Vander Ark of Denver, Colorado, has designed an excellent, creative solution to this problem. He recognized that many of the urban poor were unable to see a doctor when they had some minor health problem because of the prohibitive cost of office visits. The minor problem then became major because of the lack of timely preventive medical attention. So he organized a network of doctors who agreed to volunteer two or three free office visits a week for the urban poor. He also set up a secretary to schedule these visits. This program has proved to be so successful that Dr. Vander Ark is now starting a prenatal and pediatric clinic along the same lines. He has acquired a building in the community of need, and a group of pediatricians, obstetricians, and nurse practitioners volunteer a few hours a week to staff the clinic.

Many of CCDA's member ministries have started health care centers that can attend to all basic medical emergencies not requiring the expensive technology found only in hospitals. An affordable fee is charged for services. Often local nurses and doctors are recruited to volunteer some time, and full-time staff with a vision to serve the poor are hired at below-market salaries.

Ultimately, the only solution to the health care crisis will be a national system of health care. It will be a challenge to design this system so that it does not turn into a huge, ineffective bureaucracy and so that it allows people to choose which doctors will treat them. Such a system should be developed so that local enterprises can supply the clinics and local people can be employed; after all, health care involves a lot of money and resources, and those resources should be put to work to develop the community. It is important that there be a measure of community input and control over its health care provider.

## Security

Fear of criminals and distrust of the justice system are real problems in urban areas. A local neighborhood watch in partnership with the police force is a good way to take community responsibility for each other's property and safety. By forming this watch group, the residents are effectively declaring war on indigenous crime. Community meetings with both residents and police are important to this partnership. The residents can explain to the police why they do not feel adequately protected, the police can suggest ways to improve home security and emergency communication, and together they can think of creative ways to fight crime.

Distrust of police exists because of a history of conflict between police and ghetto dwellers, particularly minority ghetto dwellers. I would be the last one to deny that there is a long history of police abuse of blacks, and as the 1991 beating of Rodney King by the Los Angeles police department illustrates, it is not over. However, we cannot allow that history to prevent us from building good relationships with the many honest police officials and departments around the country. I believe that if we make friends with our police force—both the leaders and the officers who patrol our blocks—we will be able to hold them accountable for serving their constituents as they should. If we are in constant conflict with the police, we will be unable to deal with crime in our neighborhoods. We need to determine the good and just officers on our local police forces, make friends with them, and through those relationships bring loving pressure to get rid of those who abuse their power.

## Recreation

Most juvenile crime begins when kids have nothing constructive to do with their leisure time. If there are not already good recreational programs in the community, we need to design some. If there are, but they are not being used, we need to find out why, and address whatever obstacles there are. For example, parks often fall into gang hands, so little children don't want to play there. One solution would be to arrange for a combination of parent and police supervision of the parks so that everyone would feel free to use them again.

George Terzian, one of the Harambee board members who has been with us from the beginning in Pasadena, is the basketball coach at Pasadena City College. He persuaded us to put up a basketball hoop behind Harambee, on our parking blacktop (recently we added a fully lighted outdoor court). This is one of the best things we've done for the neighborhood. There are kids playing basketball at Harambee every afternoon and every weekend that we open it up. Teenagers and adults from the community also come over after dinner and play whenever we open the gate. They knock on Derek's door to ask if they can play basketball. Basketball has been a great way for our kids to learn the self-discipline and cooperation needed to play a team sport, as well as to let off their energy.

Encourage Christians from local churches to volunteer at the local YMCA/YWCA or Boys' Club; these places usually have excellent programs but are understaffed. Also, it is good to have a Christian influence in these community-based places. If there is no such local recreation center, look for a building in the community that could be used and recruit volunteers from the community and the church who will commit themselves to running a regular recreation program. Ask the local kids and residents what activities they would like and try to find people with the skills to direct those activities. If there is a church sports league in your area, see if a community team could join it or if the local church teams would include their neighbors on their teams.

## Beauty

What are some ways to bring beauty into the urban community of need? The first thing to do is to discover the beauty already there and promote its development. For example, in urban communities many youth have musical talent and are motivated to develop it but lack training and direction. Church volunteers could be brought in to provide music lessons for these youth. Volunteers skilled in the ethnic music of the neighborhood would be particularly valuable. Training could culminate in a community concert; as local talent is increasingly recognized and trained, a regular monthly or weekly performance could be given. Many communities are developing mass choirs, recognizing that choirs are a good way to bring people together to accomplish a common task, develop their talents and self-discipline, and enjoy themselves. The best of these choirs may be able to go on tour, giving their members further pride in their own accomplishments. Ted Travis at Neighborhood Ministries in Denver is an accomplished vocalist. He has built a music room and recording studio into his center and encourages inner-city youth to develop their musical talents.

Similar approaches apply to the other arts, such as dance and drama. Some communities have been able to take the creativity formerly expressed in graffiti and devote it to producing spectacular murals. Arts and crafts opportunities in our Harambee after-school program give the kids a chance to use artistic skills.

Take a slow walk through the neighborhood and look for the particularly beautiful gardens. See if these gardeners would be willing to teach a gardening workshop you sponsor three times each year. Time the workshops to fit seasonal planting and ask the local gardening store to provide discounts on certain items for workshop participants. They will appreciate the patronage and you will be supporting a local business.

In all of these different programs, as well as whatever programs you design for your own local community, take advantage of the human resources of the church, both in the community and the suburbs. If someone is willing to volunteer his or her time and skills, look for a way to put that skill to work to serve a felt need of the community. When you know of a felt need, challenge the church's professionals with skills that could meet that need to come forward. The church includes people from all walks of life—accountants, university professors, nutritionists, investors, police officers, teachers. Tell them that you need them to be stewards of their skills and time as well as their money and give them something they can do with those skills.

In conclusion, I want to emphasize again that a program is only as good as its ability to serve local people in their concrete circumstances. It must ultimately be from the people, for the people, and by the people to succeed. Also, the goal of these programs should be to develop your neighbors, and part of that development is giving them leadership. Encourage them to lead even if they feel a little uncomfortable doing so. Support them, allow them to make mistakes and to recover from them, and encourage them to shape the programs to serve local needs in ways that you might not have thought of doing. Finally, remember that programs are dispensable, but people are not. Developing good relationships with your neighbors is the most important thing you can do in Christian community development.

I was able to leave Mendenhall because I struggled together with the local people there, and there was local leadership that carried on the programs after I left. I was able to leave Jackson because there was local ownership of the programs there as well. Now, I see the same local leadership developing in Pasadena, and it makes me excited. Local leadership is the most important sign that long-term community development is really taking place.

# 10

# ECONOMIC DEVELOPMENT

The motto of community development in the 1960s could have been this: "Give people a fish and they'll eat for a day." The 1970s motto could have been: "Teach people to fish and they'll eat for a lifetime."

The 1970s model was a marked improvement. It removed the church from the role of provider and put the generation of wealth in the hands of community people once job skills were in place. It took a long-range view rather than focusing only on the immediate need and put into practice the American ideal that hard work generates wealth.

Neither of these approaches alone, however, can meet the enormous challenges of the urban poor today. The fact that young men felt no remorse for torching businesses in their own community during the Los Angeles riots indicates how little was at stake in their eyes. I imagine they would have felt differently if these businesses had been owned by neighbors, family members, and friends.

A more basic issue affects the economic development of urban communities. The 1990s (and beyond) approach to development needs to ask the question: "Who owns the pond?"

Economic development begins with developing people. We need to let children know in kindergarten that their education is preparing them for the day when they will have jobs. We need to explain to them that they are developing their skills and their work habits, that what they are learning now will influence the quality of their adult lives. Economic development begins with developing skills and work habits in people. You then teach them that economic development is managing what you own. What you own first is yourself, so you need to turn yourself into an asset that is valuable to others.

So economic development then becomes asset management. Asset management finally grows into developing an enterprise that you own. The challenge for Christian community-based economic development, then, is to enable the people of the community to start local enterprises that meet local needs and employ indigenous people.

In my opinion, neither the 1960s statement nor the 1970s view was adequate even for its time. They did not advance the economic well-being of the urban centers. If anything, the 1970s view only created more unskilled workers who could be hired by business enterprises at minimum wage. If the people who control the American labor system were convinced that employment would solve the urban poverty situation, they would train every adult with an employable skill and then raise the minimum adult wage level to a point where any full-time employed adult would be able to adequately support his or her family. Many authorities argue, however, that this plan would put too many companies out of business. In other words, if people were paid a livable wage, business could not survive. So training people to take minimum-wage jobs and lobbying to increase the minimum wage is not a viable option.

## Home Ownership

An important way to help people turn themselves into valuable assets is to make home ownership possible. Many businesses start when people take out loans against the value of their homes. Most of the wealth of middle- and working-class people is invested in their houses. A house can also be sold after a period of appreciation to generate more wealth. When children inherit houses the opportunity for economic strength in the second generation is greatly increased.

In places like Pasadena, it is becoming almost impossible for young people to buy houses. Habitat for Humanity provides one alternative; churches and community groups should also work to make home ownership affordable to low-income families.

There are many excellent models of such efforts among the members of the Christian Community Development Association. One is the Family Development Program of Voice of Calvary Ministries in Jackson, Mississippi. In 1986 VOC president Melvin Anderson began to walk the streets of one of Jackson's most deteriorating neighborhoods. The smell of sewer waste from a gully running next to the street permeated the air. Row after row of boarded-up duplexes ran down either side of the street. Melvin watched as drug users openly smoked crack purchased in front of the store at the end of the street.

Melvin dared to picture a whole different community on these streets. Now if you walk down Pascagoula Street you'll see beautiful single-family homes. Whole houses have been torn down to make room for yards, playgrounds, and gardens. The smelly stream has been brought under control and the streets are freshly paved. The store where dozens of people once milled about in the middle of the afternoon drinking and selling drugs has been purchased, and as a beautiful two-story Family Life Center, offers programs and services to the neighborhood.

Most important, inside the houses on Pascagoula Street are families who have realized their dream of owning a home. They attend monthly seminars in budgeting, home repair, conflict resolution, and crime prevention.

Home ownership programs like Voice of Calvary's are crucial to developing an economic base in poor communities. The poor are often forced to move due to sudden rent increases or because they are unable to pay the monthly rent. The security of a stable home gives families freedom to focus on other priorities. When the urban poor acquire real estate, they begin to take a greater interest in the well-being of their community; if they may be forced to move at any moment, they are much less likely to invest themselves in the neighborhood. They can begin to lobby for better parks, libraries, police care, fire and road services, and schools; and because they are property owners, their voices will more likely be heard. Even this lobbying is something that the poor will have to be educated to do.

## The Value of Local Enterprise

The most important stage of economic development is starting local enterprises, and I want to devote the rest of this chapter to it. What may be the greatest advantage is the role-modeling and opportunities the local businessperson can provide for the community. The example of businesspersons who can establish themselves in spite of obstacles instills pride in a community; and gradually these businesses will provide employment and learning opportunities for others in the community.

In particular, the black businessman will model a positive work ethic and integrity for black males, as he does honest, quality work at a fair price. Starting indigenous enterprises also has the advantage of keeping money within a community. At present, the economics of the ghetto are such that money generally only changes hands twice in the inner city—coming in and going back out again—rather than staying in the community for any appreciable time to make economic development feasible. This is because there are few locally based enterprises into which local residents can put their money.

Starting up a business in today's society may seem like an impossible task for a young person from the ghetto, especially since he or she is likely to lack capital, education, and political connections. But the great advantage that developing indigenous enterprises has is that the inner city is a fertile ground for starting enterprises because there is so little business in the inner city.

If a young person from the ghetto wanted to start a business in a major city's business district, the odds would be very great against that person's even being able to get started, much less succeed, since capital, education, and connections are crucial. Christian community development does not focus on developing downtown business districts, however. These areas are already developed. We want to develop the inner city and provide it with an economic base. This same young person has a very good chance, given the right support structures, of making his or her business go in the inner city, if the service or product offered meets a need in the community.

Much less capital is needed to get a business started in the inner city, simply because property values are lower. This is helped by the new concept of enterprise zones that a number of cities are starting in their low-income areas. The idea of the enterprise zone, first developed by Jack Kemp, was that a city could designate an area where it wanted business to grow as an enterprise zone; businesses that settled there would get tax breaks. At first, this concept was used by cities to develop their downtown areas. Now, however, many cities are using the same idea to develop enterprises in poor areas, with the additional requirements that the businesses are to employ local people and provide services or products that meet local needs.

A motivated and skilled person can start up a business in the community without as much education or as many connections because there is less competition and because the community is likely to support the business of a person they know. Education and connections definitely help, however, and can often make the difference between success and failure. This is where outside churches need to be involved.

Businesses in the inner city will develop best if they can draw on the resources of Christian businesspeople interested in putting their knowledge and connections at the service of local business development. If a person from the inner city who wants to start a business can find, through the church, a mentor who is established in that same area of business, that mentor can advise the new business owner in running a successful business. The mentor's own business can provide an example of a well-run business and may also be able to connect the new owner with suppliers or other important contacts. Finally, the mentor can observe, encourage, and evaluate the new owner as the new business develops.

Churches can support these businesses by using their services. The American church is a wealthy institution; I think it is very appropriate for churches to use their wealth in ways that will bring about economic development. One of those ways is to provide necessary customers to a new business. Churches can also help businesses raise capital that might not be available from a bank. Many churches invest large amounts of money. Why not invest it in businesses that are part of community development?

## A Model of Economic Development

One of the most effective examples of inner-city-based business development I know of took shape in my mind as an impossible dream: to locate a business in a declining area that would sell a viable product, employ only people from that community, be led by community people, have a surplus of money at the end of each operating year, and not use any government dollars in the process. An impossible assignment, you say, but Thriftco of Mississippi has done that since 1985—beyond my wildest dreams.

Thriftco of Mississippi is a retail clothing store with its main store in one of Jackson's low-income neighborhoods. Its board of directors is made up of area residents. Thriftco owns four stores. The main store is the size of a football field, with two other buildings alongside used as warehouse space. Thriftco also provides clothing to an additional six locations throughout the state of Mississippi on a wholesale basis. Thriftco's own stores employ twelve full-time people; its distribution network provides an additional twenty-four jobs.

It's easy to see an enterprise as exciting as Thriftco and underestimate the years of sacrifice, mistakes, and failures behind today's success. We started Thriftco in 1979 when we bought an old lumberyard with two buildings and two acres of land. The buildings were renovated with help from volunteer groups. Ours was not the traditional "thrift shop" vision. Our product was new clothing—extras and slightly damaged overruns donated by manufacturers. After repair and washing, their "waste" became Thriftco's first-rate merchandise.

My original vision was to set Thriftco up as a cooperative. During the 1960s, I had helped to organize many successful co-ops, and I felt they were a powerful means of putting ownership into the hands of the poor. Community residents were able to buy Thriftco shares at five dollars each. These shares entitled buyers to a 15 percent discount with every purchase and dividends from the profits at the end of each year. The problem was, there was no profit, and there were no dividends.

After five years of operation and nine managers, the store was $250,000 in debt. It became the manager's regular duty to fend off the bill collectors. Thriftco's board seriously considered liquidating and closing the operation. After much agonizing discussion, the board decided to give it one more try and hired Babs Salu as general manager in 1985.

The store was converted from a cooperative to a non-profit corporation. This allowed Thriftco to receive donations directly from the private sector, with a tax write-off to the donor. While the store had previously received donations indirectly from a large retail chain store and other stores, now it could receive the donations directly and on a regular basis.

A tight record-keeping system was implemented, an annual budget was made and followed, and some radio and print advertising was purchased. The store was remodeled. Tile covering the concrete floors and sheetrock on the walls made the store more attractive. A better system for mending clothing was put in place. In short, an image transformation took place. The image of a thrift shop with used clothes for poor people was changed to that of a cheerful, clean clothing store with quality merchandise at affordable prices.

"This is business," says current manager Babs Salu. "Our customers appreciate the atmosphere of the store, and we are constantly looking for ways to improve the image our staff and facility project. We have a very good personal relationship with many of our customers. This is important both for the business and for ministry to other needs they may have."

In its fourteenth year of operation, Thriftco's business keeps thirty-six people employed and generates gross annual sales of around $350,000 per year. Says Babs, "We are making plans with hopes of doubling the number of customers from 150 per day to 300 plus and of increasing our gross sales." That means more jobs and a strong business in an otherwise declining part of town.

I don't claim the credit for Thriftco's success. After he succeeded me as president of Voice of Calvary Ministries, Lem Tucker tirelessly pushed Thriftco toward stronger management and had the insight to hire a sharp businessman in Babs Salu. Babs's no-nonsense approach has kept Thriftco focused on its priority goal of economic development. Mrs. Ineva Pittman, the chair of Thriftco's board since the beginning, has poured literally thousands of volunteer hours into making the business successful. Pastor Pfleuger of New Jersey first opened the supply pipelines that kept Thriftco's shelves stocked with a quality product, and for over twelve years he dedicated himself to ensuring that the flow would continue. While in Thriftco we have often been over our heads, the commitment and sacrifice of board members, volunteers, Voice of Calvary staff, and committed customers have kept the vision alive.

The end result of Thriftco is greater than I ever dreamed. Thriftco is doing "the impossible": providing quality merchandise at affordable prices in the inner city and creating leadership and employment for that community—all without a cent of government assistance.

That is economic development—developing people to develop themselves and their community.

# 11

# PURSUING JUSTICE

In my years of ministry, from the dusty byways of rural Mendenhall to the lively streets of Northwest Pasadena, different Scriptures have become very special to me. In particular, two passages about justice have been real motivators. The first is Amos 5:24 (NASB), where God exhorts those who want to be religious but who exploit the poor to "Let justice roll down like waters and righteousness like an ever-flowing stream." The other passage is in Micah 6:6, where he asks the question, "With what shall I come before the LORD and bow down before the exalted God?" Micah's answer cuts right to the heart of true religion: "He has showed you, O man, what is good. And what does the LORD require of you? To act justly and to love mercy and to walk humbly with your God"(v. 8).

Justice is close to God's heart, and ultimately justice is an economic issue. Justice is asking the question, "Who owns the earth?" Psalm 24:1 tells us, "The earth is the LORD's, and everything in it, the world, and all who live in it." Justice is being good stewards of God's earth and resources. Justice is our management of God's resources, our working to make these resources open and available to all of God's creatures. It is an injustice when access to the bounty of God's creation is controlled by a greedy few. Therefore, a central part of our mission of representing a just God is to work for justice.

Two Old Testament concepts, the Sabbath and the Jubilee, are important in understanding justice. In Exodus 20:9, it says, "Six days you shall labor and do all your work, but the seventh day is a Sabbath to the LORD." Leviticus 25, the description of the Sabbath and the year of Jubilee, gives a thorough explanation of right relationships between rich and poor that God expects from his people.

This call to justice leads us first and foremost to work to help people come to know this good God, the God of all creation, whose primary concern is that people know him and that he is good. Then we are to help people become workers together with God, working with their own hands. Finally, we are to enable people to enjoy the fruits of their own labor and then raise their hands in praise of God. The American versions of slavery and sharecropping were so deplorable because they allowed greedy oppressors the unjust privilege of enjoying the fruit of another man's labor.

God emphasizes the importance of right relationships over and over again in his dealings with Israel; it is the most prominent theme of the Old Testament. God intended Israel's witness to the world to be a witness of justice. Their defense of the oppressed would make them shine as a light to the nations. The prophets told Israel over and over again that God would look mercifully upon them if they would live out the just demands of their Lord. Israel could not claim to follow Yahweh if their corporate life did not reflect the justice of his nature. Finally, Isaiah announces that Jesus, the Messiah, will come to establish justice and salvation, since Israel has failed to be God's agent of justice.

How was Israel failing? The Jews were fasting and observing tithes and the Sabbath, but they were neglecting the "true fast," which the prophet Isaiah described in Isaiah 58:5–10:

> Is this the kind of fast I have chosen,
>     only a day for a man to humble himself?
> Is it only for bowing one's head like a reed
>     and for lying on sackcloth and ashes?
> Is that what you call a fast,
>     a day acceptable to the LORD?
> Is not this the kind of fasting I have chosen:
> to loose the chains of injustice
>     and untie the cords of the yoke,

to set the oppressed free
 and break every yoke?
Is it not to share your food with the hungry
 and to provide the poor wanderer with shelter—
when you see the naked, to clothe him,
 and not to turn away from your own flesh and blood?
Then your light will break forth like the dawn,
 and your healing will quickly appear;
then your righteousness will go before you,
 and the glory of the LORD will be your rear guard.
Then you will call, and the LORD will answer;
 you will cry for help, and he will say: Here am I.

If you do away with the yoke of oppression,
 with the pointing finger and malicious talk,
and if you spend yourselves in behalf of the hungry
 and satisfy the needs of the oppressed,
then your light will rise in the darkness,
 and your night will become like the noonday.

Most of the Old Testament deals with God's just requirements linking the plight of the oppressed to the practices of the wealthy. This notion is hard for many American Christians to swallow because we Americans are the wealthiest people in the world. We are no different than the people of Israel if we are not willing to examine how our life-styles separate us from the poor. The apostle James warned the Body of Christ, not unbelievers, when he wrote:

Now listen, you rich people, weep and wail because of the misery that is coming upon you. Your wealth has rotted, and moths have eaten your clothes. Your gold and silver are corroded. Their corrosion will testify against you and eat your flesh like fire. You have hoarded wealth in these last days. Look! The wages you failed to pay the workmen who mowed your fields are crying out against you. The cries of the harvesters have reached the ears of the Lord Almighty. You have lived on the earth in luxury and self-indulgence. You have fattened yourselves in the day of slaughter. You have condemned and murdered innocent men, who were not opposing you.

[James 5:1–6]

## Using Wealth to Advance the Kingdom

If the issue of how our wealth is linked to others' poverty makes us defensive, we will find it hard to do Christian community development. What is encouraging, however, is that if our own wealth can be a source of the problem, it can also be a solution to the problem. Christians are called to use their personal wealth to advance the kingdom and to bring about justice and development.

The call to justice is not a demand for the redistribution of everyone's wealth so that all citizens have equal assets. Instead, the concept of stewardship tells us that Christians should not accumulate wealth without regard for its impact on others. God created us with the motivation to care for ourselves, our families, our neighborhoods. The desire for a peaceful life-style, a reasonable amount of financial security, and a healthy community environment are God-given desires. If the love of God dwells in us, then the Holy Spirit will prompt us more and more to be concerned that everyone will have those desires met. We will not be content to live in comfort while others suffer; instead, we will try to use our resources in ways that will enable all God's children to have their basic needs met.

Some Christian leaders have opposed the biblical notion of justice because they confuse it with Marxism or communism. This is a naive reading of biblical justice. Although Marxism is founded on the principle of representing the oppressed laborer, Marx never affirmed the dignity of all people; and the communist system has never in practice defended the rights of the laborer.

Communism has clearly failed. It could not compete with the energy and motivation of free enterprise. The old Soviet communist system was unable to produce the goods and services demanded by its people. Saying that the American capitalist free-enterprise system needs some adjustments to bring about justice is not rejecting the capitalist system.

The work of justice is demanding because it forces us to ask the honest questions that God asked of Israel. But asking these questions and searching for creative answers should be an exciting and joyful thing, not a burden. We should be asking ourselves, "How can I be a better steward of what God has given me?"

We should be going to private businesses and institutions where Christians wield influence and encouraging those Christians to ask, "How can I use my position and the resources that come with this position to serve God and the poor?" We should be offering suggestions to government agencies when appropriate, and we should always speak out against governmental injustice. Ultimately, however, we cannot look to the government to solve the problems of the urban poor. Rather, we should take that as the responsibility of Christians. Christian community development is "good news to the poor" and makes the church a bright light for all the world to see.

## Practicing Justice

In 1991, I began to be burdened by the great need for a magazine that would speak specifically to the issues facing our urban centers. I could hardly sleep. When God places a heavy burden on my heart, it is difficult for me to concentrate on anything else. I was literally agonizing over the continued deterioration of our urban areas, and so when I preached one Sunday morning at a local Pasadena church, I chose the passage from Matthew 4:12–16 where the writer speaks of Jesus going to the land of the shadow of death: "the people living in darkness have seen a great light; on those living in the land of the shadow of death a light has dawned."

I explained that following Jesus will sometimes mean following him into the darkest and most dangerous places. If Jesus were to visit us today, many of us would not be able to follow him because surely he would spend much of his time in the inner cities. I mentioned my burden to create a voice for urban needs.

One of the assurances God has given us is that he will not call us to do something and then leave us high and dry. Over the years, it has been the friends God has sent to me who have enabled me to act on the burdens God has given. After that service, my dear friend Roland Hinz, a magazine publisher, invited Vera Mae and me to lunch. During the course of this luncheon I invited him to join with us in launching a magazine that would be specifically focused on our newest and most difficult mission field—the inner city. It was as if God had already prepared the way. Roland readily accepted the invitation, and with his expertise and financial support *Urban Family* magazine was launched. Now there is a voice of hope and progress for America's urban community that can bring together people of all walks of life and build up urban families.

When I think of people who are trying to practice justice, I also think of my good friend Malcolm Street of Fort Worth, Texas. One day, Malcolm was taking me to the airport, and as we were talking, he said to me, "John, I don't need you to tell me about the money I'm going to give away. It's not the money I give away that I'm so concerned about. It's the money that I keep. How do I use the money that I'm going to keep? How do I invest God's resources in a way that I can serve the poor?" I began to ask him questions about his current investments. He told me he was investing in housing. I told him about the bad living conditions in parts of Dallas, and I suggested that he use his skills in some way to help the people there acquire decent housing.

A few months later I saw him again, and he told me about the apartment complexes he had purchased in a very difficult area of Dallas. He told me that he had dedicated one of those apartments to people who had fallen on hard times. Already he had given that apartment to some women who were pregnant and unmarried. He told me how he had helped one of the women attend school. Then he told me about making another apartment available to another friend of mine, Dr. Ruben Connors, who works in a ministry with the poor in Dallas. That apartment was for visiting pastors who would come into town and need a place to live. And then he told me that he took 3 percent of his profits from these apartments and put it into a fund so that when the folks in the apartments hit on hard times and couldn't pay their rent, they could apply to this fund rather than having to move out. He was being a steward of these apartment complexes, and he was making his investments where he could serve the poor. I asked him, "How are you doing financially?" And he replied, "I'm really making money." God was multiplying his blessings as he invested in the poor.

Knowing Malcolm, I know that he does not give his resources in order to get more back. He has the gift of giving, and he has learned how to be the kind of good steward, not only with his profit, but also with his assets, who brings glory to God. He has found ways to use his assets to serve the poor.

I think of another friend of mine, Norm Nason, who owns an investment corporation. He has been a partner with me in our ministry in Pasadena. He has the gift of encouragement. He is also willing to take risks in the service of God. He has helped me over and over to buy the houses for our ministry; he is like my property advisor. For example, the owners of one house wanted $150,000 for it, but it was probably worth less than $120,000. We went through a long process of negotiating with the owners, and I called Norm over and over again for his advice. He came down and looked at the house. I had offered $115,000 for the house, and I was holding tight at that; the owner finally came down to $123,000. I called Norm and said, "What should we do?" He told me that the seller would probably accept $120,000, so I made the offer of $120,000. Just as Norm had said, the seller accepted. I wouldn't have known how to get that house without Norm's advice. Norm uses his skills to help those of us who are working in the trenches practice justice. That house now has become a home for five young women who have just come out of prison, helping them get back on their feet.

George Comfort is one of the board members of Harambee. George grew up a poor boy in Watts. A few years ago, his business enterprise was listed as the ninth most profitable black enterprise in California. This business started as a small electrical supply business; everyone predicted it would fail because it was competing with another, larger business. The man who owned the other business died, and his wife sold the business to George. She told him she specifically wanted him, a black man, to have her husband's business.

As George became more and more successful, he employed black electricians, and he did all the little things he could do to further the cause of the black community in which he had grown up. He kept looking and listening for ways that he could use his resources to further the cause of Christ. He also wanted to show his gratitude to the community he came from by giving back to it. Then he read about the Harambee Center in the newspaper and decided that he would come over and check it out, to see whether it was all the newspaper had said.

One day Vera Mae was in the office, very busy, and she didn't have any time for anyone, but a man barged his way in and wanted to look around. She showed him around, and then she came back to her desk and tried to go back to work. But this man wouldn't go away; he sat down and continued to talk to her. Vera Mae told him about the Harambee Business Club. The Business Club had been started by a young woman volunteer who worked at the Avery Label Company. She was tutoring with us, and she wondered how she could use her business skills to benefit the children in the community. She discovered that the children of the neighborhood wanted jobs, so the Business Club was started.

George was so impressed with what we were doing that he became one of our main financial supporters. Then he came onto our board. He has also provided employment for some of our young people. He is forever looking for ways that he can use his business enterprise to give back to the community some of what God has done for him. George often says to me that this is not his business, but God's business, and he is just a steward of it. Just a few years ago when he spoke to us, he challenged not only us but his own sons as well, who will inherit his business once he retires, to keep in mind that it is God's business and to be continually asking how resources can be managed for the glory of God. He and his wife, Bernadette, are an example and a model of how we as blacks should use our success to bring glory to God and to help our people.

George, Norm, Malcolm, and Roland are just four of my many, many friends who have stood by me and used their assets and skills to help out. I'm so grateful for the many men and women with "secular" skills and assets who over the years have joined with us in ministry. I am thrilled that God is continuing to raise up men and women who support us and who look for ways to use their enterprises, their assets, and their lives to serve God. These men and women are concerned with being stewards. I think of John McGill and Dave Peacock in the early days. Then, in Mississippi, I think of Victor Smith and Stuart Irby. I think of Herbert West, Roy Rogers, Bill Grieg, Jeff Cotter, Stewart Gildred, Roland Hinz, Peter and Christine Geddes, Bill Hoehn, Howard Ahmanson, Pat Myers, Gary Vander Ark, John Romer, Jerry Bacon, Jim Elam, Steve and Stan Lazarian, Betty Wagner, Jaylene Moseley, Josephine Stephens, Bill Jones, Al Whitaker, and many more. These people, as far as I'm concerned, have been lights, because they have thought about how best to use their financial success, their enterprises, and their skills to bring glory to Jesus

Christ. That is one of the unique things about democracy, about America: We have the freedom to use our resources to bring glory and honor to Jesus Christ. These people still serve as an inspiration and encouragement to me.

My hope and prayer is that many more Christians with wealth and resources will learn not to be defensive about their wealth, but to use it, their business enterprise, and the power of both as tools to build the kingdom of God by developing the poor.

# PART THREE

# OUR MESSENGER

# 12

## DISCERNING THE CALL

As I look back over my life prior to 1960, I can see how God was leading me even before I entered a personal relationship with him. My upbringing and later experiences, the search for meaning and peace, the climactic end of that search with the discovery of Christ my Lord and his will for the world, all led to a concrete call for what has become my life's work. Even so, there have been many times when I have wondered why God called me to work in Mississippi, and later in Pasadena. Many people have asked me, "How did God call you?" or "How do I find God's will for my life?" or "How do I know when or whether or not I've been called by God to do something?"

To me these questions are central to understanding God's movement in history today. One cannot overemphasize the difficulties that accompany service among the urban poor. In this third section I will address many of these challenges. First, however, I want us to look at the question of calling, because this question precedes whether or not one will end up facing these challenges.

I could never have survived the ministry we have had all these years without the knowledge of God's will and the confidence of his call on my life and the life of my family. It is my conviction that God's specific summoning to service in our world involves two steps: learning God's will and hearing his call on our lives.

## Learning God's Will

God's will is in his Word, the Bible. Learning God's will began for me when I first heard the claims of his Word on my life.

My life is much like Paul's letters. Paul usually devotes the first part of his letter to affirm Christian truth, to relay the foundations of faith. The second part of the letter concerns the practical implications of faith for daily living. The first step for me was seeing that I was lost and in sin and then trusting Christ as God's payment for that sin. But it was not until I attempted to live out what the Scriptures said that I really knew God's will. In other words, God's will is in the Scriptures, yes, but after my mind was transformed by God's Word, then the Scriptures had to be put into practice. That's when I "prove what the will of God is, that which is good and acceptable and perfect" (Rom. 12:2 NASB). A transformed mind without any practical life attached to it is worthless.

This is important, because the implication of making faith practical is that my faith in Christ is relevant to every problem, personal or societal, which I face. I meet so many people who don't think their faith is relevant to anything but heaven and hell. This idea of relevance becomes clear when we see that *God's will is summed up in the two great commandments:* to love God with all that we have and are, and to love our neighbor in the same way we love ourselves (see Matt. 22:36–40).

After I accepted Christ and got settled down in my relationship with him, he immediately called me to relate my faith to others. A principle that Jesus used over and over again was to find a need and fill it. Now, I was called to find the same need in others and fill it. For me to love others like I loved myself was to share that which had given me the deepest contentment in my own life, the good news that Jesus could live his life through me. But I loved myself in other ways than seeking out a relationship with the Lord. I loved myself enough to want a good job, a safe home, and healthy food. As I began meeting people without these basic things, I saw that God's love in me wanted them to also be healthy and not retarded. Wanting these things for them was not enough; my faith had to relate to their needs, if for no other reason than that Jesus had told me to love others like I love and care for myself.

This principle of the relevance of God's will has always been a part of this ministry. If you take all the verses in the Bible and organize them under themes, the two major themes with the most individual verses supporting them are God's hatred for idolatry and God's concern for the poor and the oppressed. When you think about it, that isn't so strange. It makes sense that if the first thing God wills is that we love him with all that we are, then his chief concern must be what happens when we don't do that and worship things instead. It also makes sense that if the second thing God wills is that men and women love their neighbors with the same love they have for themselves, then his second biggest concern must be what happens when we don't do that and damage our brothers and sisters.

So the biblical evidence overwhelmingly states that the will of God is to love him in a way that leaves no room for idols, and to love our neighbors in a way that liberates them from poverty and oppression, either spiritual or physical. Most of us don't see the commandment to love our neighbor as having anything to do with dealing with physical needs. But this is primarily because we have allowed the culture in which we live to redefine the word *love* for us. The love that we talk about now is a lollipop; it's a smile and a "God bless you!" The love of Jesus, the love he intends for us to show to our neighbors, is much tougher than this. In his first epistle, the apostle John says that our love should be of the same quality as Jesus' love for us, that we get our definition of love not from our feelings or our culture but from the cross. "We know love by this, that He laid down His life for us; and we ought to lay down our lives for the brethren" (1 John 3:16 NASB).

*God's will is plain.* We are to love him and people. But when it comes to loving people, we hedge. Jesus says, "Greater love has no one than this, that he lay down his life for his friends" (John 15:13). People say, "Sure, I'm willing to die for you." But are we willing to live for our neighbor? To love people is to spend energy and resources and time to serve them. To love people in practical ways that have impact on their whole being—their spirits, their economic situation, their health, their minds—that's God's will (Neh. 8:10; Prov. 19:17; 21:13; Matt. 25:35–40; Luke 6:38; 14:12–14; James 2:15–17).

*God's will has objectives.* And one of God's main objectives is liberation, to liberate the oppressed, to offer new and more abundant life. Here again, the theological and the practical are two sides of the same spiritual reality. As we look at Scripture, especially the Old Testament, apostasy almost always resulted in economic oppression. The Book of Judges shows that Israel's spiritual enslavement to idols resulted in their own physical enslavement by their neighbors. The prophets denounced the people of Israel when they worshiped other gods and oppressed their own brothers and sisters. This oppression always brought God's judgment, their own collapse, and sometimes captivity. A total liberation, spiritual and physical—that is the objective of God's will.

*God's will works from the inside out.* This is assumed in the order of the commandments: When we love God first with all our hearts, then we can express our love outwardly to people. That's energy! That's power! It also means that if I have not dealt practically with God's will in my life, he cannot use me as a vessel for his love to others.

Up until the time I was saved I had always interpreted my problem as an economic one. I thought, "If I can just make it in business, then I will be set." God couldn't use me to really share his gospel with my people until he had shown me how my evaluation of my need was wrong. Even after I was saved, I could have continued to assume that I had to make it economically instead of seeking God's kingdom first. If God hadn't dealt with us inside, with our values, he wouldn't have been able to use us to develop cooperatives, the health center, and other projects that express his love while dealing with people's physical needs. We would have been too busy "making it."

Finally, God's will is to work through broken vessels. When I think of heroes like Samson, Gideon, and David with all their flaws, I wonder at the way God has committed himself to shooting his power through and revealing himself in human beings. One of the really great things about God is that he arranges the broken fragments of our lives together in a beautiful mosaic that exhibits his glory. Paul knew this when he said, "We have this treasure in jars of clay to show that this all-surpassing power is from God and not from us" (2 Cor. 4:7), and "[The Lord] said to me, 'My grace is sufficient for you, for my power is made perfect in weakness.' Therefore I will boast all the more gladly about my weaknesses, so that Christ's power may rest on me" (2 Cor. 12:9). If you are a human being, it is God's will to work through you. That's Good News.

## What God's Will Isn't

One big problem I see, especially in young people who are enthusiastic about their faith, is that many ask, "What is God's will for my life?" rather than thinking about God's will, period. I have people say to me, "I want to know God's will for my life." Then I find out that they have already decided what careers they are going to pursue, whom they are going to marry, where they are going to live, how much they will earn, how many children they will have, and what kind of car they are going to buy. This happens with people preparing for full-time ministry as well as for secular vocations. It is not God's will that these people are looking for, but their own will. They are not asking, "What is God's program on earth and how do I fit in?" Their question is, "How does God fit into my life?"

We live in a society where individualism is held up in honor, where the rugged individualist is the person who makes it. Our culture, our environment, our whole teaching, are permeated with an individualism that is increased by the competition in our society. God's will, however, exists apart from us and does not depend on us or our response to him. God's will for our individual lives must be found within his overall will. It's our responsibility to find out what that will is, adjust our wills to it, and do it. As we discover God's will, we find the most perfect will for our own lives.

*God's will is not my culture.* It is not individually tailored to fit the assumptions I hold dear in life, like getting an education or going to a particular church or treating a certain group of people differently because of their skin color or their income.

*God's will does not just ratify my present life-style.* I can't know God without having to at least question and maybe change my present patterns of thought and my attitudes. Lustful desire for things, a need for personal acceptance or status, tradition, and environment—all these things can keep a person from hearing the will of God and its claim on his life. All can maintain a person's individualism and keep her from accepting the responsibility of God's work and the opportunity to be a vessel for his power (1 John 2:16–17).

## Hearing God's Call

After I know God's will in the world, I can listen for his call to ministry. God's will exists whether or not I exist or respond. It is objective. But the call of God is where my feelings, my talents, my very gut response to God makes a difference, because it is *a summons to a special place or situation in which I can do God's will with the special and unique equipment he has provided me.* As believers we can find complete unity in God's will (Eph. 4:1–6). But when it comes to our calling, the Spirit of God explodes into diversity in our midst by giving us different gifts (1 Cor. 12; Eph. 4:11–12). It is dangerous to talk about "feeling" God's will. But we are on solid ground if, knowing God's will and doing it, we are looking for the opportunity in which we can be of greatest use for the kingdom, and where we can, as a result, feel the greatest sense of personal satisfaction and fulfillment. One way to be called by God is to find out where God's will is being done in the world and get yourself there.

Other principles can help us hear the call of God. *God's call to ministry is usually a response to past faithfulness.* It is the formal commissioning of a person who is already functionally participating in God's will. We ought to be faithfully in a ministry where we are before we get "called" to do something someplace else. We begin to experience the call to ministry as we do his will. The person who is faithful in a very little is faithful also in much (Luke 16:10; see 19:17 NASB).

The apostle Paul is a good example of this. After spending a year faithfully teaching at Antioch, he then was called to continue what he already had been doing but in a way that would use all of the special equipment and training with which he had been prepared. Like Paul, we don't have to worry about being adequate to respond to God's call. God will not call us to do something that he won't equip us to do.

*God's call to ministry is perceived in unity*, first with the Scriptures and then usually with the fellowship or group of people to whom we are accountable. I have seen too many people who have angrily rejected the leadership of the Body just so they can go and do their own thing, even if it is their own "Christian" thing. I am not talking about total agreement here. The group of people I was most committed to before I left California, the Fishermen's Fellowship, did not want me to go to Mississippi at all. But they knew that I was submitting my life to them, and God's call became plain to them as they saw me and knew my gifts. Thus I could leave that local fellowship with a sense of direction and support. My brothers and sisters could trust my calling, having faith in the God who had given me the gifts.

The third principle is that *God's calling is in relationship to building his Body.* It is not the ultimate purpose of God to glorify himself through individuals, but rather through groups of people who are called by his name (Eph. 1:18; 3:10). God did not intend for me to be a lone-wolf Christian. From the time we became involved in ministry, he has provided us with people who could support and encourage us as well as hold us accountable to doing his will.

As an individual I can be a witness. But even though I as a missionary may seem to be alone, there are always others standing by me, praying from afar or working by my side. And this is a reflection of how God moves us out of our individuality toward the Body. In the Body, with all of the gifts making up the arms, legs, and other parts, we can become the actual, in-the-flesh representation of Jesus Christ, the very Body of Christ.

Paul always talks about the gifts of the Spirit in relationship to the body of believers. And I have seen this happen as God's call to us has been accompanied by his call on the lives of many others. It has been a real confirmation of my call to Mississippi and Pasadena to see others called to the same vision and work.

Finally, *there is no escaping the call of God.* Responding to the call of God is like a trap. It's like walking into a closet and shutting the door and finding out that there is no doorknob on the inside. You just can't get out. Once I got to Mississippi and began to do God's will I was trapped. Personally, I wanted to get out so much sometimes that I would have caught the first thing smoking out of town. But I couldn't leave. Before we returned to Mississippi, I had cut off my alternatives. We had left our jobs. For me to leave would have been to deny something that I knew about the character of God himself and his faithfulness. I would have had to deny some of what I knew about his will and the personal way that he finally called me.

Why were there times when I wanted to back out and leave? I guess it was because God's will was not really giving me the personal gratification that I wanted in terms of popularity and acceptance. It was really tough when we were rejected by both the black and white churches in the area. But I learned something: Once God has called you to do something and you become his person for the task, he will complete his work. God will glorify himself through you, though you are sometimes unwilling. I think of Jonah, Moses, and Jeremiah. It's a process of growth and real wrestling.

I believe in God's call, and I think it is central to making Harambee Christian Family Center what it is today. We wanted to be here; we couldn't be anywhere else at this time. We have cut off all the alternatives and have no choice but to plant our feet and be obedient. This kind of call—the kind that puts us in a box—grinds up the individualism that destroys our witness. Through obedience and submission to the people we leave behind, through calling us to use our special gifts to continue to do his will, through calling us in bodies, God's purpose is so great and we are so frail that he pens us in and ends up using us. The call was the beginning, just a taste of the grace that would be sustaining us as we laid the foundation for a work among black people in the urban areas of this country.

## The Call to Urban Ministry

There are five issues that relate to our general calling to urban ministry—issues that commonly emerge in the life of Christians considering service among the poor.

### *Motivation by Need*

It is possible for those of us who have been called and are living in the community of need, to become overpowered by the many needs around us. The need as it relates to poverty in general does not constitute our calling. It has been difficult over the years for some to understand why Jesus could make a callous-sounding statement like, "the poor you will always have with you." Isn't our job to eliminate poverty? Jesus was moved to compassion when he was personally confronted with a need. His task was not to heal every disease and feed every hungry person but to witness the presence of God in a specific place, to specific individuals, as he came in personal contact with them. It is those deeply felt needs of the individuals that move us to respond; as we live in the neighborhood, interact with the people, are moved to compassion by their felt needs, we then organize the meeting of these needs into community development action programs.

Those who would try to solve all the problems, meet all the needs, and feed all the hungry will not last long in situations like our urban centers. The needs are too many. Effective Christian community developers will find a life-style that allows them to remain Christ-centered in the midst of urgency, to slow down even with all the unmet needs around them and "pour oil on the feet of Jesus." Those who can do this will be able to draw strength for the long haul and take up the sword day after day, year after year.

### Love

While a central claim of this book is that it is not possible to be Christian and live a life that ignores the pain of the world, we must keep in focus that it is for Christ that we labor and to *him* that we give our sacrificial love.

Christians can, in fact, give themselves to the most grueling and costly forms of service, to the point of spending their lives for the poor and giving themselves to being burned at the stake. But if our acts of service are done out of some other motivation and not done in love, 1 Corinthians 13 tells us it is in vain. Our ministries, our youth programs, our health centers, our housing projects, our evangelism—all these actions must be motivated out of a love for God.

Make no mistake. It is this love for God that moves us into this neighborly action. There is no duty or work to which the Christian is called outside of the two great commands that we love the Lord our God with all our soul, mind, and strength and that we love our neighbor as ourselves (see Luke 10:27). Jesus said that on these two commands hang all the requirements of the law and the prophets. This is the essence of our Christianity. Love is the common denominator: a *love* for God and a *love* for neighbor.

The lessons that are drawn from this, concerning service and calling, are several. First, God views our relationship with him fundamentally as rooted in the love he has for us and our response of love to him.

Second, we discover in time that a maturing love relationship with God quite naturally leads to our transformation whereby we become loving persons. God's very nature is love and so our very nature becomes love. Mature Christians are unable to love God without a deep love for their neighbors. What's left for mature Christians is to find God's guidance on how love for neighbors is to be expressed.

The third lesson is that we cannot presume to earn God's acceptance through our deeds. We are accepted by him simply because we are his children. Our labors are labors *of love*, not labors to gain approval. Christian leaders who work in the inner city are often troubled by staff who are trying to earn God's love or the approval of others more than they are moved to compassion by the needs of their neighbors. We cannot hope to find our self-worth through our work. If we do we are actually using the poor to advance our good feelings about ourselves.

### A Pastoral Heart

Christians must not come to the poor as know-it-all saviors. A calling to the urban poor requires a pastoral heart because life there is painful and messy. The pastoral heart is one that is continually capable of returning to the main point of ministry: people. We may begin a ministry among the urban poor with great visions of programs we wish to implement (and may even have the funding to back up the ideas) but people—no matter where we are—will always frustrate our programs. If our service among the poor goes at a pace that does not in every facet reaffirm the dignity and priority of people, then we need to review our calling with the question: Do I really care about people? Funerals, weddings, divorces, unemployment, hospitalizations, evictions, and suicides require people who care to spend their time with people.

God instructed Moses to require Aaron, who was the model of a pastor, to wear on his robe the names of the twelve tribes of Israel. They were, in a poetic sense, a burden to his shoulders, and all his ministry was conducted with the weight of their life pressing down on him. God further instructed Moses that when Aaron was making major decisions regarding Israel he was to have a brooch over his heart on which were inscribed the names of the twelve tribes of Israel. As we serve the urban poor, they must be held in our hearts as precious before God.

## The Gifts of the Holy Spirit

God will nudge people who have a mature love for him and a pastor's heart to consider life in the inner city, and God equips people for that calling.

My perception of spiritual gifts is that they are gifts of the Holy Spirit given to individuals, as a part of the Body's call to the world. Our gifts are fundamentally linked to God's corporate calling on the church. They are the very possession of the Holy Spirit and something over which we have been made stewards. Our gifts are to bless the entire body in making God's "will be done on earth as it is in heaven" (Matt. 6:10). As we discover our gifts, we begin to ask in what unique way God has endowed us to bring others into the same love we now experience.

## Community

At the heart of Christian community development is the local church, the community of believers who are intentionally linked together in worship and service. As such, our calling to the urban poor does not express itself outside the context of a local group of people. Our gifts, provided by the Holy Spirit, belong to the church, not to us as individuals. We bring who we are to the community of faith and seek, by God's grace, to live our lives out together as an indication of the gospel at work in us—corporately. To withhold our gifts from that local fellowship is to deprive the work of the community of faith of the unique contribution we are able to bring. Similarly, to isolate ourselves from that community is to deprive ourselves of the majority of gifts we will require to faithfully fulfill the calling of inner-city ministry. The inner city is no place for a lone ranger. No, we are not linked to others in service as though we were a missing piece in a puzzle. Instead, we are linked to a living organism called the church working together in a specific location that has its own dynamic life.

So we constantly change, adjust, adapt, let go, regroup, abandon, commit, experiment, fail, and hold on. A rigid sense of self and of calling will not survive in any ministry context, especially in the difficult terrain of the urban poor. Our calling there is a process, an adventure by faith and fellowship, whereby we go from a general understanding of God's heart for the poor to a specific expression of that heart among specific people. There we discover that our gifts fit into people's lives, rather than people having to fit into our gifts; that we are part of a community; and that while we came for the sake of others, it is really for our own sakes, our own growth, that we must continue in the calling.

# 13

## COUNTING THE COST

In my experience, too many young activists have rushed into the inner city without regard for the cost. The normal, natural hardships that ensue come as a complete surprise, often leaving them embittered and cynical concerning ministry to the poor. I have often seen disillusioned, hurting activists lash out in pain at co-workers and ministries, for no other reason than, "Things did not turn out as I expected."

What are the life-style costs one can expect as a worker among the urban poor that accompany those who relocate to the places of pain? Let me say first there are many "rewards" of such a move, but I am wary of reducing such a noble pursuit to a list of benefits.

My hope is that the short "cost list" that follows can be a tool to help current urban workers understand that they are not alone in their pain. I'd also like to take a little of the romance out of soon-to-be-activists who have heard the wonderful motivating talks to make the urban plunge, but who perhaps have not listened to the Lord, who instructs us to calculate the cost of our tower before commencing construction. No doubt you will be able to add to my list.

### The Unfamiliar

"It's the toughest job you'll ever love" is the upbeat recruitment slogan that entices workers and volunteers to join the Peace Corps. Although this statement contains much truth, most of us know that it is short-sighted. Mission agencies, the U.S. State Department, and even the Peace Corps all know about one of the first and surest problems that face individuals who move to a culture that is significantly different from their own: culture shock. At first, there is this wonderful feeling of the new and refreshing lessons. People dress and eat differently, their art and music are exotic, their customs are a curiosity, and their way of communicating is so interesting. Typically the new arrival will write home about these great discoveries and describe them with gracious delight. "How could I have been so privileged to be assigned here?"

Imperceptibly, the people and their customs begin to change. This typically happens over a space of seven weeks to seven months. Now you are wondering why they don't eat "right," why they listen to "lousy" music and are so "annoying" in their relational practices. This shift is so slow that you barely notice the contrast to your initial impressions. When something goes wrong—perhaps your car is dented or a ball breaks your bedroom window—you perceive it as an "enemy" attack. "They" did it on purpose. "They" don't like you and, after all, "Here I am sacrificing for their sake." What's worse, your co-workers are not sensitive to your needs and they too, in fact, have taken on obnoxious habits. The sponsoring organization obviously does not have it together. It's time you consider moving on to a more spiritually equipped group and a more thankful neighborhood.

For Chris Rice, the temptation to leave began whispering to him when, after two years of exciting service with Voice of Calvary in Jackson, Mississippi, some of his black co-workers began to confront Chris and other whites about their attitudes of superiority and their policies and practices that put blacks at a disadvantage. "I was there to help, to give, to teach, and to do," reflects Chris, "but when the people I said I had come to serve began asking me to be helped, to receive, and to learn, that's when I began packing my bags." In the aftermath of painful confrontation, with the help of trusting friendships that began to bud with his black co-workers, Chris realized that while a "missionary" mentality is a good place to start, you can't come from the outside and hang in over the long haul without becoming more than a do-gooder. Today, because of Chris's relationship with my son Spencer, their families along with other families have formed a deep bond of trust that is the basis for their common outreach through *Urban Family* magazine, a neighborhood children's ministry, and a ministry of guidance to single mothers, ex-offenders, and young people.

Few people are entirely exempt from the forces of culture shock. It helps to know ahead of time that you will go through it, and it helps to be linked in relationship to others who are able to recognize its signs and point them out to you. In time, if you successfully adjust to your new environment, it will be the result of making much of the unfamiliar your friend, while also retaining some of your former, cherished ways—as much as your new life-style allows. Many whites who have relocated into the black community say that close personal relationships with black friends help to make the adjustments much easier.

## *Possessions*

There is no way that you can secure a guarantee for the safety of your property should you move into the inner city. You take precautions, but if you spend valuable time trying to make it impossible for your possessions to get stolen, then that is how you will spend all of your time. Drug habits lead to robbery-for-the-next-fix; unparented children whom you invite into your home will sometimes stuff their pockets with your valuables. It would be a mistake to underestimate the likelihood of burglaries and break-ins. Moving into the inner city demands that you value your neighbors and your neighborhood above your possessions. They will get stolen. It is helpful to take inventory of everything you bring into your new location and mentally review the possibility of robbery. You should not keep items that you're unwilling to lose. This is not to promote a defeatist attitude concerning safety of possessions nor to suggest an accepting view of burglary, but it is one of the realities you face with life in the inner city.

Robert Lupton says we need to realize that we have been trained to marry our possessions to our value system, and so letting go of the things in exchange for people is not as easy as it may at first appear:

> Preserve and maintain. Conserve and protect. They are the words of an ethic that has served us well. Over time these values have subtly filtered into our theology. It is increasingly difficult to separate the val-

ues of capitalism from the values of the kingdom [and in the purely secular sense—from the values of what's "right" about the American way]. Stewardship has become confused with insurance coverage, with certificates of deposit, and protective coverings for our stained glass. . . . Somewhere on the way to becoming rich we picked up the idea that preserving our property is preferable to expending it for people.[1]

### Security

I do not want to deny the increased danger that comes with specific urban settings. Fierce drug competition, gang rivalries, and other activity related to lack of juvenile supervision catches too many innocent people in between. The tragic violence brought against peace-loving citizens is reprehensible and criminal no matter what conditions lead to it—be they turf battles or natural consequences of poverty. Urban workers must understand that they are not exempt from these occurrences. The Scriptures say the rain falls on both the just and the unjust.

On the other hand, while random acts of violence do happen, the vast majority of violent crime involves lovers, people involved in the drug trade, and people who have chosen a dangerous life-style. There are exceptions, and it is probably these exceptions that are the cause of our greatest heartache.

Marcia Reed and her husband Phil, a pastor at Voice of Calvary Fellowship Church, have lived more than fifteen years in Jackson, Mississippi's inner city. One night, while Phil was away doing the Lord's work at a state prison two hundred miles away, Marcia was attacked in bed in her home by a man who had broken in through a window. We thank God that Marcia was able to scream loudly and fight back, causing the man to run out of the house.

In the aftermath, Marcia struggled with fear and anger, haunted by roaming imaginations of the mind. *Where did God go?* she asked as she wrestled with her pain. *Why did he let this happen? How do I deal with being so afraid of the night?* With the help of the strength and love of her husband, plus the loving arms of people in her church, Marcia began to find comfort and peace. Marcia knew many women in her neighborhood who had experienced similar and even worse situations. "But most of them," she says, "because of limited economic options, had no choice but to stay and work through their pain. My emotional ups and downs needed to be dealt with right where God had called me to be a witness for his kingdom."

"Where was God that night?" she asks. "He was right there, watching over our family, teaching me to trust him even with my very life, giving me strength to endure, and even more, to now use this experience to comfort and encourage others who have answered the same call for the glory of his kingdom."

Marcia wrote in CCDA's newsletter, the *Restorer:*

> I am not the same person I was when I went to bed that night. I am weaker, but stronger in the Lord; less adequate to deal with life, but more willing to trust the Lord with my life; still insecure about the danger of the inner city, but more secure in the people that God has surrounded me with. As weakness has become an opportunity to show God's strength, it has reinforced our family's conviction that we are right where he wants us to be.[2]

### Emotional Pain

Many aspects of urban ministry are emotionally draining and demanding. Urban activists are likely to be barraged with the entire spectrum of human need. The emotions will be taxed beyond normal experience and in time, one is likely to become exhausted, depressed, and even despairing. The cause is not usually clear to the activist and so despair is compounded with feelings of inadequacy and doubt. This syndrome leads many people to give up on urban service. Normal pressures such as parenting, earning an income, repairing a flat tire, and restoring a damaged relationship, all take on massive proportions that are not a real reflection of the actual pressures themselves. The emotional drain related to all the caring can make even the smallest challenge a formidable task.

It is key to have all of our giving supported by close, trusting relationships. Sensitive friends will be able to discern the onset of emotional drain, provide support, carry some of the burden, and offer helpful counsel on means to revitalization. The demands of this environment tend to place themselves on the new worker more directly and forcefully. Pulling away has to be planned and implemented almost as a discipline until new (and unconscious) recreation patterns replace the former.

In the final analysis, cost counting must be weighed against God's call on your life. If he has, indeed, called you to a difficult place, remember that he has promised that wherever he takes you, he will never leave or forsake you. He has promised to fill us with the hope that he can make a difference through us. As my friend Wayne Gordon is fond of reminding those in the trenches of Christian community development, "Remember: It ain't easy, but it can happen."

In the Summer 1990 issue of the *Lamppost*, my son Spencer addressed this issue of the costs of an inner-city calling. "One of the major concerns of Christians interested in inner city ministry is the safety of their families. 'Will we be safe?' This is a very relevant question especially in light of all the 'war stories' (various stories of crime). First of all, that question is very subjective. What is safe? If we are talking about our personal physical safety, then the answer is a qualified yes. There are very few accounts from inner city Christians of their people being physically hurt or killed. But if we are talking about whether or not our 'stuff' will be safe, that of course, is another matter."

He continues. "The question 'Is it safe?' brings to mind a scene in C. S. Lewis' classic story, *The Lion, The Witch and The Wardrobe*. In this particular scene, the Beavers are describing to the children the Mighty Lion, Aslan (the Christ figure), who has 'called' the children to meet him at the Stone Table (symbolic of the Cross). The Beaver's awesome description of the great Lion made the children hesitant to go, and prompted one of the children to ask this same question: 'Is He safe?' The Beaver's response to this question rings true to us that are called to follow Jesus into the inner city. 'Safe?' asked the Beaver. 'Who said anything about safe? Of course He's not safe, but He's good.'"

# 14

# URBAN SERVANTS

God's call to service *for* my life cannot be separated from God's intention to work *in* my life. When we approach a community primarily as givers, and not also as receivers, we miss the most of what God intends through our service. This is the wonderful economy of God. All serving goes both ways: outward and inward. God's change agents are continually in the process of being changed themselves. The quality of our service cannot be separated from the quality of our character.

I see this life-style of giving and receiving as something that a person grows into. When God calls people to the inner city, he often takes them through a growth process where he accepts their service as well-intended do-gooders, and shapes them into mature, effective urban servants.

## The Caseworker

When God first grips your heart for the poor and you move into action, it's an exciting moment of high and noble purpose. Those who first confront the needs of the inner city come with exhilaration pounding in their hearts, eager to impact lives with their gifts and passion. Their eagerness and energy are great strengths. I call these fresh troops *caseworkers:* They view their role as one of helping, giving, and making a difference in the lives of others.

This is a good place to start. We decide to take a step out of our own world and do something because we know God is concerned about the poor. We're motivated by compassion; we want to help, to meet a need, to accomplish a task that will glorify God. We have training, skills, and resources that are needed.

Some of us organize a work group or volunteer some time or decide to give regularly to an inner-city ministry. Those who take these steps play a vital role in bringing Christ to our cities. Others of us go beyond that. We see the need for leadership and provision of new services. Someone needs to step out decisively and get things started.

The key commitment needed at this initial stage is to truly serve those you have come to help. One volunteer group from a suburban church with only limited exposure to the poor thought after only a few days that they knew more about solving inner-city problems than people who had lived and worked there for many years. One black woman, trying to give them a taste of local "soul food," was treated rudely and insulted for her attempts. It made me wonder why they came to us instead of going to Disney World.

The problem with this group was that they were willing to serve only as far as their private agenda extended. They had come to do something for the poor, but they weren't willing to listen and learn from the very people they thought they were serving. They wanted only to tell and do. Often caseworkers—as compassionate as their motives are—want to dictate when, where, and how they will help, instead of asking what is needed.

I have worked with countless eager beavers over the years who have proclaimed God's call on their life and can't imagine what could be better than serving in the inner city. However, as well-intentioned as they are, as important as their resources are, their superior technical skills and formal education often come prepackaged with a sense of what poor people need. They are reluctant to adjust their predetermined formula for success and have difficulty listening to people who are "less educated." They don't recognize how much they lack the street experience, relational expertise, understanding of the community, leadership skills, and simple faith of indigenous people. Without these qualities, in fact, technical resources make little long-term impact. With no mutually vulnerable exchange of ideas, caseworkers view indigenous people more as their "caseload" than their peers. People in the community quickly pick up on these attitudes.

Recent Bible school or seminary graduates find it especially difficult to go into the urban poor neighborhoods as learners. Their education often leaves them with an inflexible view of mission. And even someone native to the community of need can bring a caseworker mind-set. After receiving formal education, often they return to their community assuming they have a mandate to lead, feeling that their education and race give them that right. While the very goal of Christian community development is to see such leaders come back into the community, there is a need for these people to serve the community first, before earning the right to lead.

Effectiveness can also be undermined by supporting churches and individuals. If investors and supporters are impatient for results, undue pressure is put on the efforts of those at the front lines. When supporters have a short-term mentality—when they want to know just how far their money has gone, how many people have been won to Christ, what leaps the gospel has made since the previous prayer letter—the worker is pressured to give up a long-term focus in order to satisfy the donor. Supporters do make missions possible and offer some accountability, but they, too, must be reeducated as to the hard, long-term reality of urban life and missions.

While a passion to do good and to help is where God often starts us, eventually you must make an attitude adjustment to grow beyond being a caseworker. All too often, when the pain of this adjustment sets in, once-passionate missionaries hear the mysterious call to go somewhere else.

The decision to move beyond being a caseworker involves a commitment to identify, build, and serve godly indigenous leadership. When you come to the inner city with your resources and skills, gird yourself with the towel of a servant and wash the feet of the godly people who have made a commitment to live and minister there. You will only be effective as you come to these relationships willing to learn, listen, and serve.

## The Convert

When you make the commitment to be more than a giver and to be a receiver, too, you begin to move from the role of caseworker to that of *convert*. I use this word because becoming an effective urban servant is sort of a conversion process that is often ignited by painful confrontations with the people you have come to serve. Through these experiences, God begins to purify our motives, humble us, and bring us face-to-face with our need to grow. As you admit your need for growth, you begin to understand how you need the indigenous people as much as, or even more than, they need you. Several steps of learning are important in this "conversion" process of becoming effective urban servants.

First, urban servants learn the importance of trusting relationships with people from the community. A basic problem prevents "insiders" and "outsiders" from developing close relationships: lack of trust. Year after year, people in poor communities have watched politicians make promises, suburbanites whoosh in for two hours of passing out tracts, and tent revivals drop in for a weekend, never to return. They've seen outsiders come and go, always giving their input and advice, even though they would be gone long before the full consequences of their decisions would be evident. The burden is on those coming to help to take the initiative in relationships, to understand, and to be patient. Building trust begins with developing trusting relationships with people in the community, both natives and long-term transplants, who can talk honestly to you, teach you, help you understand the culture, and confront you if necessary.

Second, urban servants learn the need to support godly local leadership and to contribute to its further development. An important test for any work of ministry is whether or not it develops indigenous Christian leadership. Many outsiders come to the urban community primarily to provide services, which are often desperately needed. However, we must remember that just as Jesus' strategy was to make disciples, our bottom-line focus should be on working with local leadership to develop disciples of Christ who love God and their neighbor. As these disciples mature spiritually and sharpen their leadership and technical skills, more responsibility should be passed into their hands, for they are the most effective leaders in redeeming their communities.

Sometimes, if we're willing to make the necessary life-style sacrifices, we may be called to start new structures—health centers, businesses, youth programs, and housing ministries. But outsiders should continually seek out godly local leadership that they can partner with. It's easy to put program efficiency over people development, which is a long-term process whose fruit will only be borne after investing many years into people.

Third, developers learn to use their gifts in a servant role. Even those pioneering in ministry often buy into a value of upward mobility that our culture takes for granted. Philippians 2:5–7 expresses the Christian counter-ideal: "Your attitude should be the same as that of Christ Jesus: Who, being in very nature God, did not consider equality with God something to be grasped, but made himself nothing, taking the very nature of a servant, being made in human likeness." Downward mobility was the way of Jesus and should be our way, too.

When faced with the need to put the development of local people over the development of their own gifts, outsiders often begin packing their bags. Often we are more concerned with our own "rights" than we are with true reconciliation and development. The cost of giving up some of our own personal skills and development is too high a price to pay. If we're called to serve in an urban community, we're called to use our gifts in a way that puts local needs above our own.

Fourth, urban servants learn to see the ways the gospel is alive among the poor, taking on forms that seem foreign because of limited exposure. Certain Scriptures perhaps never had any significance to you, but in a context where near-orphans roam the streets because of gang warfare and family breakdown, you find the intense heart of God to be the Father to the fatherless. In this encounter you discover people who have uncovered a vulnerable God who is restless to parent the orphan. You are made richer for the experience of learning.

There are many godly people in urban communities who are truly "poor in spirit," whose simple faith and experience of suffering have taken them to a depth of relationship with God that goes well beyond your own encounter with Christ. As Robert Lupton puts it from his own experiences of learning from the poor: "So it was that God's children who suffer most from crushing poverty became the very ones God used to speak to us of our own spiritual poverty."[1]

Fifth, urban servants come as learners of urban society. You make it your business to understand all you can about urban society's richness and pain: its history, politics, economics, myths, handed-down stories, religious experiences, hardships, and achievements. You read its poetry and novels and listen to its philosophers (many who on the outside look like town drunks are actually the best articulators of our community's philosophy). The entire complex web that makes up this unit of society becomes of genuine interest to you.

Justice For All (JFA), a group of white Christians based mostly in Iowa, is a great example of Christians who are willing to come and serve the inner city in any way that the indigenous people see fit. Each year they send out over two hundred people to go into poor areas all over the nation and to use their skills to support the ongoing works of the kingdom there. Their servant attitudes are not only refreshing, but they have deeply impacted those they work with. Each year, their acts of service challenge us to be more Christ-like in our own work among the poor. JFA is a model example of people who are giving a great deal, but who have been deeply changed by God in the process through their relationships with people in the inner city. They are true models of converts.

So if you are called to the urban poor, to be effective, you must eventually become a learner and a servant. Serving is not a means to an end; service itself is the high, dignified calling to which the gospel aspires and to which men and women captured by that gospel aspire.

## The Comrade

For some, the call of God on your life will take you still deeper. Some of us are called to live among the poor, whether that means leaving suburbia, making the decision to stay in the inner city, or going back to the poor community where you grew up. Those who answer that call of commitment develop a very special and mutual relationship with the poor; the poor community becomes their home; the needs and interests of the inner city become their very own. These people I call *comrades*. You see, God's love is very personal and down to earth. To demonstrate his love, he took the form of a man: "The Word became flesh and dwelt among us" (John 1:14). Jesus joined in our suffering, identifying completely with us (Heb. 2:14–18). As we unite our interests, our families, and our homes with those we come to serve, a deep bond develops with our neighbors. We begin to have more and more of a personal stake in bringing justice to our communities, in seeing it change not just for the benefit of others but for ourselves.

Herb and Sarah Myers were part of Voice of Calvary for ten years, where Herb served as a doctor at the VOC health center. In 1990, after a painful decision to leave Mississippi to further their training in the fields of psychiatry and occupational therapy, Sarah shared some reflections: "In relocating to a poor community I began to share the struggles and problems of my neighbors. An inadequate educational system is not just their problem, it is now mine too. Crime and gang activity threaten our family as well as theirs. When landlords refuse to repair their homes it affects the value of ours. This morning as Herb and I jogged through three miles of our neighborhood, we passed Mr. Howard who is a resident in one of the many personal care homes in our area and a patient of my husband. A big smile spread across his face and he greeted us with a cheery 'Good morning, Doctor Myers!' I had the feeling we had added some happiness to his day just by being part of his world."

Becoming comrades is a step toward mutual submission between outsiders and indigenous, those educated on the streets and those educated in universities, transplants and natives, black and white and brown: "Submit to one another out of reverence for Christ" (Eph. 5:21). Together we begin to shape a local unit of interdependence and accountability: "We . . . form one body, and each member belongs to all the others" (Rom. 12:5).

Through the rich comrade relationships that are the result of this service, God will truly bless you. I am who I am today because of all of those people in Mississippi who, though financially poor, shared their lives with me, made me their comrade, and shaped me into what I am today.

I am who I am today because brother Isaac Newsome of New Hebron, Mississippi, who had been teaching a Sunday school class for over thirty years, humbly turned over that class to me and helped make me an instant leader within that community. I am who I am today because Mr. Buckley, a simple farmer and the smartest man I ever met in my life, shared his life with me and discipled me. I am who I am today because Nathan Rubin, a Simpson County civil rights leader, led the group that protected my home at night when the Ku Klux Klan was threatening to burn down my house and kill me and my family.

When I think of each of these people, I remember the words of the apostle Paul, "And the things you have heard me say in the presence of many witnesses entrust to reliable men who will also be qualified to teach others"(2 Tim. 2:2 NASB). Those faithful men taught me, and it has become my responsibility to find other faithful people and to share with them the good news about Jesus Christ.

Now I live with a sense of burden because of everything those men who were poor in spirit shared with me and taught me. When I think about my own commitment to the poor I think about those men, and if I should slow up, if I should procrastinate in seeking justice for the poor, I would feel like I was letting those men down. All their lives, these men were in need of the kinds of things Voice of Calvary Ministries, Mendenhall Ministries, and the Harambee Christian Family Center have to offer. These kinds of relationships lead our service to become more than an idealistic endeavor. They become actions on behalf of and in partnership with people who have become like family.

As you commit to urban servanthood, the deeper you go, the more you will realize the great paradox of servanthood: While we are called to die to our selfish interests, it is not until we have put our own interests at stake that we can become full partners—white and black, rich and poor, indigenous and transplant and volunteer—in ministry. "From him the whole body, joined and held together by every supporting ligament, grows and builds itself up in love, as each part does its work" (Eph. 4:16).

Comrades learn from one another and help each other grow. Reshaped through the purifying and refining of the convert process, those who have transplanted themselves make a positive and vital contribution. At the same time, the need for local indigenous leadership doesn't diminish but intensifies as we recognize firsthand the need for visible, strong leadership relevant to the aspirations and needs of the black community.

## The Call for Encouragers, Investors, and Volunteers

Throughout this book I have stressed how living among the poor is at the heart of the strategy of Christian community development. Making the decision to move in, or to stay if you are already there, or—if you left—to go back (perhaps after vowing never to return), is a calling from God. Many more Christians and their families must respond to that call to "go" if our urban communities will ever be turned around.

While some are the front line troops, others have an important role to play on the supply lines. Those not living among the poor play a vital role in building up urban communities. But remember: It's important that you affirm that those living among the poor are the most effective urban servants. Your resources, skills, and expertise gain in effectiveness the more they are channeled through godly indigenous leadership.

One of the most important roles on the supply lines is volunteers. We have been enormously blessed by volunteers throughout our ministry, first in Mississippi and then in California, and the volunteers have been blessed in the same way. I am always meeting men and women who came down to Mendenhall and Jackson when they were young who say to me, "The time that I worked with your ministry really helped shape my life." Volunteers are a vital part of any Christian community development ministry, and it is important for volunteers to understand their role within the community and within the ministry.

It is very important for volunteers to come ready to support the indigenous leadership in the community. White people and college students especially often come into the community and have a hard time submitting to the authority of the indigenous leadership. It can be very hard to submit to authority when you feel that because of your education you could do a better job if you were in charge.

Volunteers need to believe that the people with the problem might know best how to deal with the problem, and it takes humility to accept that. Very skilled and very talented volunteers come through the Harambee Center all the time, and one of the first lessons they all learn is that they have not lived in the community long enough to know what needs to be done. Volunteers must learn to ask, "How can I follow you?"

If you live near the community of need, the possibilities for what you can do as a volunteer are endless. Many ministries in the Christian Community Development Association have some sort of after-school tutoring program. You might volunteer one night a week to tutor a child. At Harambee over fifty volunteers weekly tutor in our tutoring program. Quite a few of these volunteers have been coming for many years, and in that time they have developed positive, influential relationships with a child or a particular group of children. Cliff Briggs, a Harambee board member, and his wife Lorie have established a relationship with an entire family—the Garcias. Just this year they had a part in convincing one of the Garcia boys to go to college. Some volunteers help out for specific activities, like Christmas parties, weekend camping, horseback riding, and trips to the theater. Because most of our children come from broken homes, some volunteers invite children into their homes to demonstrate to them what a loving family is. In the summer many volunteers are needed to run summer programs. Each summer twelve to fifteen volunteer summer interns come to Harambee, live in the community, and teach in our summer day camp.

You might volunteer as part of a work group. I would say that most of the labor for many of the building projects we have completed over the years was done by volunteer groups from around the nation. Our work groups come and work on whatever project we have going at the time. It is very important that a work group come to help fulfill a need that has already been defined by the indigenous leadership in the community. When Harambee purchased a former drug house on our block last year, we had a series of work groups paint the house, put up a wood fence all around the property, and clear away debris.

There are so many other ways that you can support the CCDA ministries that I cannot list them all here. Harambee is blessed to have so many people who joyfully make their consistent contributions. Pat Myers of suburban La Canada Presbyterian Church, who is also the founder of Caring Churches of the Foothills, brings us good, day-old bread and pastries every Friday that would otherwise be wasted. Sally Damon-Ruth, who lives in our community, bakes cookies weekly that are eaten by the children following Good News Club every Tuesday. George Luna, a plumber and handyman, comes by every few months and fixes the little things that aren't working quite right. My dear friend Dorothy Ertel spends extra time at Harambee just before our annual banquet, helping us to prepare for it and also helping arrange travel for me and my staff. Susan Long is another wonderful homemaker who donates one day a week doing whatever we need her to do.

Not only can you offer your gifts and skills for a time, but you can bring your new understanding and vision back to your home church and help them to shape a meaningful Christian response to the cries of the needy. I consistently find that those churches that respond most compassionately to the needy are those that have sent out from their own congregations people to live and walk and eat and breathe among the poor, and who have then heard their eyewitness accounts of the need, the opportunity, and the challenge.

Since we have been in Northwest Pasadena, Lake Avenue Congregational Church has been a wonderful partner to the Harambee Center. Many of our volunteers come from this church, which is located two miles away. When we do neighborhood surveys we go to one of their Sunday school classes and recruit volunteers to help us, and our surveys are completed in a day's time. They have graciously shared their church facilities with us. Many of my dearest friends are a part of that church.

Christian businesspeople have a special role to play in Christian community development. You might help support the development of business in the community by committing not just your resources but your own time and skill. Many of our young men who are starting out in business have not had the benefit of growing up in business families or the opportunity to get formal business education and therefore do not have a deep understanding of how businesses function. Established businesspeople can come alongside these indigenous businesspeople in mentor relationships. Many leaders of inner-city ministries are drawing upon the expertise of Christian businesspeople as board members to help oversee the operations of the ministry.

No matter what God's call is on your life, whether you are called to be on the front lines or the supply lines, I urge you to commit yourself beyond charity to holistic Christian community development. Come alongside the urban poor; treat them as you would your own family. Jesus, as he hung on the cross, said to John, "Behold, thy mother"(John 19:27 KJV) and to Mary, "Behold thy son"(John 19:26 KJV). The urban servant comes alongside the people, feels their felt needs, works for holistic development, and receives and gives to the community of which he or she is a part. The volunteer comes in and submits to the authority and the leadership of the indigenous leaders. Working together, we can become the manifest Body of Christ, keeping the faith that was once for all delivered to the saints.

# 15

## FACING THE CHALLENGES

The work of Christian community development is a deeply spiritual endeavor. If we lose sight of that, our efforts are in vain. Jesus said, "I am the vine; you are the branches. If a man remains in me and I in him, he will bear much fruit; apart from me you can do nothing" (John 15:5). Without being grounded in a living relationship with Christ, our presence will be short-lived, our vision short-sighted, our motivations impure.

The call to bear fruit among the poor is birthed within the family of faith, joins together in a specific location, and matures through the belief that God will begin to communicate his agenda in that context. There is the waiting, the listening, the expectation that God will move in the presence of people who submit themselves to his rulership. There is the conviction that God goes into the world ahead of our efforts, desires, and creativity.

In this chapter, I wish to highlight specific spiritual battles that the Christian community developer will have to fight. There are others, but these are the spiritual struggles that we most typically encounter when choosing to stand with the oppressed urban poor. To fight those battles, we must begin in humble openness before God.

### Beginning in Prayer

Effective ministry begins in prayer. The ideal prayer is, "your kingdom come, your will be done on earth as it is in heaven" (Matt.

6:10). We need to ask, "Lord, what would you have me to do?" Prayer should not be an excuse for inaction but a preparation for action.

I remember when God called us here to Northwest Pasadena. I had gone to dinner with Dr. Paul Cedar, who at that time was the pastor of Lake Avenue Congregational Church, and I began to share with him that we felt God was calling us to this area to make a difference. He responded, "What can I do to help?" I told him I would be so grateful if he would send some men to help me. So he sent George Terzian, Roland Hinz, and Steve Lazarian, all solid Christian men and dear brothers. Others, including Jerry Bacon and Steve and Gladys Jackson, joined with us and together we prayed every Monday night for our direction in the neighborhood.

This ministry on the corner of Howard and Navarro was born in prayer. I remember one night, as we were praying together in the back room, we heard shots outside. We ran outside and found a thirteen-year-old boy who had been gunned down on the street with his pockets full of dope. He had been selling dope on the wrong street corner. Our hearts were knit together that night. These friends of ours who started with us nine years ago are still with us today. So you can see why I say this ministry was born in prayer. Just recently we have started again a "community" prayer meeting where we join together with believers from the neighborhood on Thursday evenings for prayer. Christian community development must be anchored in prayer.

Prayer is not a means to secure God's blessing or approval for our plans, no matter how noble or charitable they may be. Our prayers are to tune us in to what God already has planned. We pray because we realize that our struggle is not against flesh and blood but against principalities and powers. We dare not perform outside that reality.

## Suffering

Suffering is the way God's power is known. "My strength is made perfect in weakness," says the Lord. The suffering Christ on the cross of Calvary was the means by which God completed the cosmic battle against Satan. That moment was the climax of a heavenly struggle that handed the victory to Almighty God. Jesus was whipped, mocked, beaten, nailed, pierced, and buried. Yet he won. The road to victory is paved with sacrifice.

We will find ourselves on our knees many times praying our Lord's very own prayer: "Father, if it is at all possible, please remove this cup from me. Nevertheless, your will be done"(see Matt. 26:39). It is a spiritual dynamic that every significant work of the kingdom brings suffering. We are told that one day these trials will pass, that there will be a day where there is no crying. But that day is not yet here. We certainly may avoid the challenge of spiritual suffering, to some degree, by staying away from the places of pain, but then we will be betraying the blood of Christ that had to be shed on our account.

Take heart from the Scriptures when you find yourself in the center of affliction. Know that you are not alone and lean on the community of faith to support you:

> Others were tortured and refused to be released. . . . Some faced jeers and flogging, while still others were chained and put in prison. They were stoned; they were sawed in two; they were put to death by the sword. They went about in sheepskins and goatskins, destitute, persecuted and mistreated—they wandered in deserts and mountains, and in caves and holes in the ground.
>
> [Heb. 11:35–38]

> Dear friends, do not be surprised at the painful trial you are suffering, as though something strange were happening to you. But rejoice that you participate in the sufferings of Christ, so that you may be overjoyed when his glory is revealed.
>
> [1 Peter 4:12–13]

If we are not encountering suffering, then how could it be the cross of Christ that we are carrying? There have been many times in my own life when I encountered suffering because of the stand that I was compelled to take for the sake of the gospel. One of the darkest moments in my life was my experience in the Brandon jail, where I was beaten within an inch of my life by hateful highway patrolmen. But God in his sovereign wisdom has turned that dark experience into one that shines brightest for his glory. God used that night to instill in me the urgency of preaching and living a gospel that burns through all the barriers that separate people from each other.

## Brokenness

Being broken is one of the consequences of suffering. Urban developers will discover after a time that they are not only depleted of spiritual and emotional resources, but they will feel nearly crushed and in a state of disrepair. Their self-image will weaken, their sense of strength will diminish, and doubts will crowd their minds as they face limitations where before there were only wide open horizons of opportunity. The Scriptures say that we are cracked vessels. The light of Christ in us is able to shine through those cracks. We have to go through the wrenching experiences of brokenness to understand this principle, but once we experience it we will discover that Christ calls us to minister in his strength, by his Spirit—not by our might or power. In our brokenness we will face the cruel onslaughts of the evil one who will come to accuse and condemn us in our pitiful state, but in time we will be able to appropriate the truth that God does not despise a broken and contrite heart (see Ps. 51:17).

## Failure

Those just beginning in ministry often look at Mendenhall Ministries, Voice of Calvary Ministries, and Harambee and comment on the great success of these ministries. I know better. I could write an entire book on all the failures, mistakes, dead ends, and defeats along the way to establishing these ministries. The effective urban servant is one who is able to bounce back, to keep pushing in spite of the odds.

We will stumble and fail along the way. Our purest motives and sincerest efforts will not protect us from failure. We need to mentally accept this ahead of time. We must go through the fiery trial of failure before we are able to fully accept the fact that failure "comes with the territory." In this struggle we will confront the cultural value of success. Says Robert Lupton: "Success is not an automatic consequence of obedience. 'A righteous man falls seven times and rises again' (Prov. 24:16). Saint and sinner alike must take their lumps and go on to the next risk. But for the believer there is one guarantee. We have a dependable God who made a trustworthy commitment that no matter what happens—success or failure—He will use it for our ultimate good."[1]

Because my view of Christian community development is not simply an idea of manipulating variables until we are able to produce a satisfactory outcome but rather a spiritual endeavor in a dynamic, changing environment that offends the aggressive kingdom of darkness, I expect that battle will produce wounds and defeat along the way. As the apostle Paul tells us, we may be bashed about in every form imaginable but ultimately we are not crushed. If the enemy takes us on, he has engaged Jesus in conflict. And the Scriptures tell us that the battle belongs to the Lord.

For those who hold fast to a long-term vision, failures can become stepping stones to the difficult task of developing people. Lem Tucker, the president of VOC Ministries before he died in 1989, used to say that there were too many people "with a fifteen-year agenda and a two-year commitment." Even the most successful ministries in Christian community development will not really begin to see the fruit of ministry until ten or fifteen years of committed work have passed.

I wish that at my funeral it could be said that I have fought the good fight, that I have finished the course, that I had kept the faith, and I would like written on my tombstone, "I tried." I may not have succeeded, but I tried.

## Faith and Hope

Because our battle is ultimately spiritual, we cannot enter the ministry of urban work without employing our faith. We have to reach outside our own resources and depend on Christ to fit us for the work. Those who enter the work of urban ministry out of a confident sense of their own resources and qualifications will have a difficult time.

The thrust of my ministry has been *community*. My vision has been to develop a group of people committed to racial reconciliation through the church. This work can't be "just a job." You can't pay people enough for them to dedicate their souls to a cause like this.

It simply doesn't work to go outside the community, solicit résumés, and hire leadership.

We enter ministry fully expecting that God will have to work *for* us and *through* us. Indeed, we suspect that if his presence does not go with us then we will refuse to go. We will not be surprised by our intense need of God's regular intervention on our behalf. In fact, we will begin to doubt our calling if our knees are not bruised from the pleading of our prayers.

Connected to this faith is a hope, not a hyped-up positive attitude kind of hope, but a secure sense that if we give ourselves in faith to the service of the King, good will result for the kingdom. Our prayer, "Thy kingdom come"(Matt. 6:10 KJV) is an active exercise of hope. Those who have worked among the urban poor know the degree to which despair can suffocate the poor and those who work with them. "Things will not change" is a village fact of life, and this despair feeds itself and leads to even greater despair.

I have found Paul's exhortation in Philippians 4:8 a source of motivation for me and my staff as we face the difficulties of urban spiritual warfare: "Whatever is true, whatever is noble, whatever is right, whatever is pure, whatever is lovely, whatever is admirable—if anything is excellent or praiseworthy—think about such things." I have found that negative people sap my strength and that of others around them. One of our favorite songs at Harambee is called "Nothing's Impossible," and I believe we are called to be a people who believe deeply in the hope that when God's people take action, we can affect the outcome.

We come with hope—not a hope expressed in energetic, motivational language and pep talks, but a quiet, gentle long-range look that doggedly works for the kingdom in spite of all the external evidences that would call for despair. Perseverance is the friend of hope. It does not insist on continued effort because of human strength and cultural values. Rather, perseverance keeps us going because it is convinced that hope is right. Our message, our very life should be good news to those who despair.

## Loneliness and Rejection

Jesus was rejected by his homeboys after his first sermon. They even threatened to throw him off a cliff (see Luke 4:14–30)! Talk about getting off on the wrong foot! All urban developers will at some point go through desperate periods of aloneness—dark times when no one seems to understand or care, when God is too distant to understand, when our best efforts are judged as useless and our sincerest attempts are judged as ill-motived.

One of those times for me was my contemptible trial in 1971. As I sat in the courtroom, I could feel the despair all around me. I was on trial for inciting the people of Mendenhall, Mississippi, to stand against the injustice and oppression that had been their lives for so many years. But according to some, I was overstepping my bounds as a minister of the gospel. As I sat there during the long and exhaustive ordeal, I felt all alone and unappreciated. Did anyone care what I was trying to do?

The more I listened to the angry insults and lies, the more I began to despair even though deep down I knew I was right. It was as though Satan were weaving a web of darkness all around me that was about to snuff me out and my gospel with it. But during one of the recesses God sent to me an angel of hope. She came in the form of a little old black lady. As I stood there in the hallway, my countenance low and my shoulders drooped, she gave me a simple message of inspiration and hope that must have come from God. She looked me squarely in the eyes and said in her quivering, broken dialect, "Stand up, son—stand up."

For me, those simple words were enough to inspire me to go back into the court and continue the fight. Even though none of the physical circumstances had changed, I now felt stronger. The old lady and her words told me that I was not alone, that I was fighting a spiritual battle, and that God and his people were with me.

There is no alternative to these times. They develop our character and mold our calling. We have to go through a sifting process whereby God alone is the object of our desires, passions, and motives to serve. This process culminates in the refiner's fire, where all the impurities are painfully burned from the metal until eventually there is the prize of pure, undefiled gold. I say these words not as one who has acquired this undefiled status but as one who is still being tried by the fire.

We do, of course, have One who has gone before. Jesus was despised and rejected. He did not manage his aloneness as super-God. No, he asked the disciples three times to stay awake with him as he pled for mercy. He screamed out in agony, "My God, my God, why have you forsaken me?"(Matt. 27:46), while the crowds looked on in shame and mocked this pitiful, naked criminal who went about claiming to be God. Three times he asked his friend Peter, "Do you really love me?"(John 21:15–17). Denied that love at his most vulnerable hour, Jesus pursued their friendship even after his resurrection.

Christian community development will demand the full exercise of our faith, our hope, and most of all, our love. All three will be taxed to their very limits. But the good news is that we will experience the full reward for having faced that spiritual challenge, not only in heaven, but as Jesus says, there is no one who has left the comforts of life for his sake who will not receive much more in this present age and in the age to come, eternal life (Matt. 19:29, paraphrased).

# 16

## "WHOM SHALL I SEND?"

Throughout this book I have intentionally limited my use of the most important single word that describes Christian community development. I have avoided the word for fear that its familiar ring would leave the work of Christian community development itself powerless to communicate. That word is *incarnation*. Christian community development takes this old theological word to new depths and heights.

Incarnation in its simplest form is the reality and promise that, we, by our very presence, personify Jesus. The disciples walked with Jesus and then heard the final instructions that they were to go into the world as Jesus had been sent. Incarnation is the life of Jesus continued in a community, through the church. I alone cannot be the Body of Christ. *We* are the Body of Christ. In every conceivable way, incarnation is a social event—it is public, it happens in a concrete circumstance, its work is determined by the environment of need, both spiritual and physical. Its sensitivity is informed by the history of pain; its evidence is transformed lives on location; it is a confrontation in the public square between the forces of those who would destroy and those who would love. It is worship, marriage, and family at peace. It is neighbors reconciled and at rest. It is despair turned to hope, and it is dignity not bestowed but affirmed. "The Word became flesh and made his dwelling among us. We have seen his glory, the glory of the One and Only, who came from the Father, full of grace and truth" (John 1:14). The incarnation strives for no less than Jesus living through us, so that others too will touch, feel, and see with their own hands and eyes the glory of the Father.

Perhaps the crowning moment of Christ's incarnation is where we find God Almighty weeping—weeping because his life has become so linked to the pain of others that he is broken.

In the words of Bob Pierce, founder of World Vision, "May my heart be broken by the things that break the heart of God." The time for holistic Christian community development is now. Charity is not enough. It falls far short of Christ's example and cannot embody the whole person of Jesus Christ.

Now is also the time for reconciliation. In the sight of God there is no such thing as a "black" or "white" church. The thought of this kind of separation and alienation because of race, I believe, leaves a bitter taste in the mouth of a just and holy God. We, the Body of Christ, must be that reconciling agent in the world. We must sit down together, learn to trust, to pray, to move and rescue our ghettos.

The Christian community development movement has taken for its theme verse Isaiah 58:12. These words are our marching orders: "And those from among you will rebuild the ancient ruins; You will raise up the age-old foundations; And you will be called the repairer of the breach, The restorer of the streets in which to dwell."

When the prophet Isaiah came into the presence of God all he could say was, "Woe to me! . . . I am ruined! For I am a man of unclean lips, and I live among a people of unclean lips, and my eyes have seen the King, the LORD Almighty"(Isa. 6:5). But God in his mercy reached down and touched Isaiah and forgave his sins. Because of God's act of love, Isaiah felt responsible. Once touched by God, Isaiah then heard his Master's call on his life, "I heard the voice of the Lord saying, 'Whom shall I send? And who will go for us?'" Isaiah's response should ring true for us who have similarly been touched by a just and holy God. He could give no other response, and because of what God has done for us, we can give no other response: "Here am I. Send me!"(Isa. 6:8).

# APPENDIXES

# Appendix A

## RESOURCES

### Books

Bakke, Ray. *The Urban Christian*. Downers Grove: InterVarsity, 1987.

Castro, Emilio. *Sent Free: Mission and Unity in the Perspective of the Kingdom*. Grand Rapids: Eerdmans, 1985.

Claerbaut, David. *Urban Ministry*. Grand Rapids: Zondervan, 1984.

Costas, Orlando E. *Liberating News: A Theology of Contextual Evangelization*. Grand Rapids: Eerdmans, 1989.

Greenleaf, Robert. *Servant Leadership*. New York: Paulist Press, 1977.

Jones, William. *God in the Ghetto*. Elgin: Progressive Baptist, 1979.

Kehrein, Glen, and Raleigh Washington. *Breaking Down Walls*. Chicago: Moody Press, 1993.

Lupton, Robert. *Theirs Is the Kingdom: Celebrating the Gospel in Urban America*. San Francisco: Harper, 1989.

————. *Reweaving the Fabric: A Radically Realistic Approach to Urban Community Development*. Atlanta: FCS Urban Ministries, 1993.

Nouwen, Henri. *In the Name of Jesus: Reflections on Christian Leadership*. New York: Crossroad, 1991.

Perkins, John. *Land Where My Father Died*. Ventura, Calif.: Regal, 1987.

————. *Let Justice Roll Down*. Glendale, Calif.: Regal, 1976.

————. *With Justice for All*. Ventura, Calif.: Regal, 1982.

Perkins, Spencer, and Chris Rice. *More Than Equals: Racial Healing for the Sake of the Gospel.* Downers Grove: InterVarsity, 1993.

Snyder, Howard. *The Problem of Wineskins: Church Renewal in a Technological Age.* Downers Grove: InterVarsity, 1975.

Steele, Shelby. *The Content of Our Character: A New Vision of Race in America.* New York: St. Martin's Press, 1990.

Sullivan, Leon H. *Build, Brother, Build.* Philadelphia: Macrae, 1969.

Wallis, Jim. *Agenda for Biblical People.* New York: Harper and Row, 1976.

Weary, Dolphus. *I Ain't Comin' Back.* Wheaton, Ill.: Tyndale House, 1990.

## Magazine

*Urban Family.* P.O. Box 40125, Pasadena, CA 91104.

## Videos

Bakke, Ray. *The City for God's Sake* (3-part series), MARC.

———. *God Is Building a City,* 2100 Productions.

Perkins, John. *The Church's Responsibility to the Poor,* Gospel Light.

———. *Cry Justice,* Gospel Light.

———. *The Felt Need Concept,* Gospel Light.

———. *Leadership for Today,* Gospel Light.

# Appendix B

## CHRISTIAN COMMUNITY DEVELOPMENT ASSOCIATION

God's people at the front lines among America's poor are finding refreshment and discovering that they are not alone through the Christian Community Development Association (CCDA). CCDA is a church-based movement of over 175 ministries and churches active among the poor in 75 cities and 30 states. Its mission is to develop a strong fellowship of those involved in Christian community development. New and existing members are supported and encouraged.

CCDA's membership is interracial and its leadership is heavily drawn from America's minority communities. One of CCDA's most important distinctions is that most of its members live in the very communities where they are involved. The members of CCDA are united in their belief that people empowered by God are the most effective solution for the spiritual and economic development needs of the poor.

CCDA was formed as a direct result of the John M. Perkins Foundation for Reconciliation & Development. Since its beginning in 1983, the Foundation has focused on joining people of need with people of resource. As many sound Christian community development ministries began sprouting up across the country, the Foundation called these organizations together, and in 1989 these ministries formed an association for the purposes of mutual encouragement and expanding the work of Christian community development.

CCDA has adopted a definition of Christian community development:

> "Reconciled Christians working together mobilizing spiritual and physical resources in and for communities of need through the Church in a community-determined way that is redemptive."

The following key objectives guide the efforts of CCDA's members:

- Encourage and promote fellowship among Christian community developers
- Facilitate the exchange of information among existing Christian community development organizations
- Serve as a clearinghouse for Christian community developers with needs, linking them with those possessing the needed resources
- Train people in the philosophy and skills of Christian community development
- Educate and mobilize the Body of Christ at large to become involved in Christian community development in their area
- Enable and equip communities in need to start new Christian community development organizations

CCDA offers the following benefits:

- Networking: Through CCDA, you will benefit from the knowledge and experience of others at the front lines of ministry
- Annual convention: Every year CCDA practitioners from across the country gather to exchange ideas and fellowship together
- Access to institutes and training centers: CCDA offers training in Christian community development through regional institutes and community-based training centers
- Clearinghouse service: Screening and directing of request for information

- *Restorer* newsletter: Each issue highlights CCDA issues as well as new laws, program ideas, biblical teaching, and "how-to" articles
- Organizational and phone consultations
- Job referral service
- Annual membership directory

CCDA offers two different memberships:

Individual member: Annual dues—$5 student, $20 individual, $30 husband and wife

Organizational/Church member: Annual dues based on funded gross annual income—$50 under $300,000; $100 between $300,000 and $799,000; $200 for $800,000 or more

To become a member, contact CCDA and ask for an application.

CCDA
3848 West Ogden Avenue
Chicago, IL 60623
Phone: (312) 762-0994
Fax: (312) 762-5772

# Appendix C

## ORGANIZATIONS

The following organizations, all members of the Christian Community Development Association (as of October 1992), are working in poor communities across America. Contact the ministries in your area for more information about how you can get involved.

**Alabama**

The Center for Urban Missions, Birmingham

**Arizona**

Restoration Ministries, Phoenix
Seeds of Hope, Casa Grande

**Arkansas**

Serving to Equip People, In the Name of Christ (STEP), N. Little Rock

**California**

Bayshore Christian Ministries, East Palo Alto
California Recovery Facility, Oakland
Christian Believers, Richmond
CityTeam Ministries, San Jose
Discover the World, Pasadena
(The) Downtown Church, Fresno
Evangelicals for Social Action, Fresno
Gilead Group, Oakland
Harambee Christian Family Center, Pasadena
Harbor House E. Bay Ministries, Oakland

John M. Perkins Foundation for Reconciliation & Development, Pasadena
P. F. Bresee Foundation, Los Angeles
San Francisco Leadership Foundation, San Francisco
Sonoma County Christian Network, Inc., Santa Rosa
Vineyard Christian Fellowship, Pomona
World Impact, Inc., Los Angeles
World Vision, Monrovia

**Colorado**

Christian Corps International, Denver
Community Outreach Service, Denver
Compassion International, Colorado Springs
Hope Communities, Denver
Mile High Ministries, Denver
Neighborhood Ministries, Denver
Young Life's Multiethnic & Urban Ministries, Denver

## District of Columbia

Servant Leadership School

## Florida

Christian Resource Center, Tampa
Our Savior Lutheran Church, Miami

## Georgia

FCS Urban Ministries, Atlanta
Koinonia Partners, Americus
MAP International, Brunswick
Mission to North America, Atlanta
Perimeter Ministries, Inc., Atlanta

## Illinois

Agape Community Center, Chicago
Bethel New Life, Chicago
Breakthrough Urban Ministries, Chicago
Chicago Lawn Alliance Church, Chicago
Christian Friendliness Association, Moline
Christians Helping Inspire Local Development, Lake Bluff
Circle Christian Development, Chicago
Circle Urban Ministries, Chicago
Cornerstone Community Outreach, Chicago
Douglass-Tubman Youth Ministries, Chicago
End Times Youth Evangelism Enterprise, Chicago
Faith United MB Church, Chicago
Inner City Agape Ministries, Chicago
Inner City Impact, Chicago
Jerusalem Christian Development, Chicago
Lawndale Christian Development Corporation, Chicago
Lawndale Christian Reformed Church, Chicago
Lawndale Community Church, Chicago
Mid-America Leadership Foundation, Chicago
National City Ministries, Wheaton
Near North Conservative Baptist Church, Chicago
Oakton Community Church, Evanston
Restoration Ministries, Harvey
Riverwoods Christian Center, St. Charles
Rock of Our Salvation EFC, Chicago
Roseland Christian Ministries, Chicago
Salem Evangelical Free Church, Chicago
Spirit of God Fellowship, South Holland
Wheaton Youth Outreach, Wheaton

## Indiana

Christian Fellowship Church, Evansville
Community Fellowship Ministries, Indianapolis
Impact Ministries, Evansville

## Iowa

Community Bible Church, Clive
Good Samaritan Urban Ministries, Des Moines
Justice For All, Rock Valley

## Louisiana

Desire Street Ministries, New Orleans
Trinity Christian Community, New Orleans

## Maryland

New Song Community Church, Baltimore
Newborn Holiness Church, Baltimore

## Michigan

Christ Church, Grosse Pointe
Christian Community Development of Jackson, Jackson
Christian Reformed World Relief Committee, Grand Rapids
Church of the Messiah, Detroit
Church of the Messiah Housing Corporation, Detroit
Empower, Detroit

John 3:16 Ministries, Albion
Joy of Jesus, Detroit
Rosedale Park Baptist Church,
  Detroit
Spring Arbor College, Jackson
Wellspring, Detroit

## Minnesota

Park Avenue Urban Program and
  Leadership Foundation,
  Minneapolis

## Mississippi

Antioch Community, Jackson
Canton Bible Baptist Church, Canton
Mendenhall Ministries, Mendenhall
(The) Myers Foundation, Inc.,
  Tchula
Quitman County Development
  Corporation, Marks
Voice of Calvary Fellowship, Jackson
Voice of Calvary Ministries, Jackson
Young People in Action Ministries,
  Jackson

## Missouri

Are You Committed, Kansas City
Fellowship of Urban Youth, Kansas
  City
Independence Boulevard Church,
  Kansas City
Kids Across America Kamp, Branson
National Conference for Pioneering
  Black America, Wentzville

## Montana

Montana Rescue Mission, Billings

## New Jersey

Life Line Emergency Shelter,
  Trenton

## New York

Refuge Temple Church, New York

## North Carolina

Building Together, Inc., Raleigh

## Ohio

Because He Cares, Akron

Christian Outreach Ministries,
  Mansfield
Community of the Servant, Dayton
Living Word Love Center, Cincinnati
Operation Jochebed, Akron
Rhema Christian Center, Columbus
Teens Against Pre-Marital Sex,
  Cincinnati
Urban Concern, Inc., Columbus

## Oklahoma

Hope Outreach Center, Enid

## Oregon

Restoration Community Church,
  Portland

## Pennsylvania

Beaver Falls Youth Network, Beaver
  Falls
Center for Urban Theological
  Studies, Philadelphia
Diamond Street Community Center,
  Philadelphia
Eastern College, St. Davids
Fleischmann Memorial Baptist
  Church, Philadelphia
Good Works, Inc., Downington
Philadelphia Leadership Foundation,
  Philadelphia

## Tennessee

Memphis Leadership Foundation,
  Memphis
(The) Resource Foundation,
  Nashville
Urban Community Vision, Knoxville

## Texas

Common Ground Ministries,
  Waxahachie
Oak Cliff Bible Fellowship, Dallas
Reconciliation Outreach, Dallas
Voice of Hope Ministries, Dallas

## Virginia

Broken Chains International,
  Chesapeake
Christian Communication
  Technology, Virginia Beach

Project Light, Virginia Beach

**Washington**

Covenant Housing Association,
  Seattle
Emerald City Outreach, Seattle

Family Life Ministries, Tacoma
Northwest Urban Ministries, Seattle

**Wisconsin**

Eastbrook Church, Milwaukee
Elmbrook Church, Waukesha

# NOTES

## Chapter One  Beyond Charity

1. David Claerbaut, *Urban Ministry* (Grand Rapids: Zondervan, 1984), p. 132.
2. Shelby Steele, *The Content of Our Character: A New Vision of Race in America* (New York: St. Martin's Press, 1990), p. 28.
3. Steele, *The Content of Our Character*, p. 34.
4. Robert Lupton, *Theirs Is the Kingdom: Celebrating the Gospel in Urban America* (San Francisco: Harper, 1989), p. 78.
5. Not its real name.

## Chapter Two  From Quick Fixes to Felt Needs

1. Lupton, *Theirs Is the Kingdom*, p. 46.

## Chapter Three  The Marks of an Authentic Church

1. Orlando E. Costas, *Liberating News: A Theology of Contextual Evangelization* (Grand Rapids: Eerdmans, 1989), p. 69.
2. Richelieu Richardson II, "This Ain't Right," *Urban Family*, Spring 1992, p. 34.
3. Leon H. Sullivan, *Build, Brother, Build* (Philadelphia: Macrae, 1969), pp. 42–43.
4. Costas, *Liberating News*, p. 134.
5. Lupton, *Theirs Is the Kingdom*, p. 91.

## Chapter Four  The Living Gospel

1. Costas, *Liberating News*, p. 20.
2. Costas, *Liberating News*, p. 9.

## Chapter Five  The Burden of Proof

1. Howard Snyder, *The Problem of Wineskins: Church Renewal in a Technological Age* (Downers Grove: InterVarsity, 1975), p. 22.
2. Jim Wallis, *Agenda for Biblical People* (New York: Harper and Row, 1978), p. 33.
3. Wallis, *Agenda for Biblical People*, pp. 33–34.
4. William Jones, *God in the Ghetto* (Elgin: Progressive Baptist, 1979), pp. 68–69.
5. Snyder, *The Problem of Wineskins*, p. 172.

## Chapter Seven  Evangelism

1. Costas, *Liberating News*, p. 18.
2. Emilio Castro, *Sent Free: Mission and Unity in the Perspective of the Kingdom* (Grand Rapids: Eerdmans, 1985), p. 17.
3. Costas, *Liberating News*, p. 22.
4. Costas, *Liberating News*, p. 79.

## Chapter Eight  Wholesome Care

1. Claerbaut, *Urban Ministry*, p. 17.

## Chapter Thirteen  Counting the Cost

1. Lupton, *Theirs Is the Kingdom*, p. 9.
2. Marcia Reed, "Inner-City Danger," *Restorer* (Fall/Winter 1992), p. 7.

## Chapter Fourteen  Urban Servants

1. Lupton, *Theirs Is the Kingdom*, p. xi.

## Chapter Fifteen  Facing the Challenges

1. Lupton, *Theirs Is the Kingdom*, p. 78.